POPCORN & PEANUTS

by
Julianne Lemon

Illustrated by Mike Nelson

©Copyright 1977
Nitty Gritty Productions
Concord, California

A Nitty Gritty Book*
Published by
Nitty Gritty Productions
P.O. Box 5457
Concord, California 94524

*Nitty Gritty Books — Trademark
Owned by Nitty Gritty Productions
Concord, California

ISBN 0-911954-40-6

Library of Congress Cataloging in Publication Data

Lemon, Julianne.
    Popcorn and peanuts.

    Issued with the author's Peanuts and popcorn;
inverted text.
    Includes index.
    1. Popcorn. 2. Cookery (Peanuts) I. Title.
TX803.P35L46 (TX799)   77-2408
ISBN 0-911954-40-6

Table of Contents

The Popcorn Institute and American Pop Corn Company have generously contributed recipes and information for this book. We thank them.

The Popcorn Story

It may seem like a trivial snack to you—but popcorn has a past that might astound you. As one of the world's oldest, as well as most distinctive foods, it is an important item in the story of mankind. There is now no doubt that the original corn was popcorn and it is quite probable that the first use man made of corn was by popping.

Archaeological research indicates that long before Columbus popcorn had spread to all Indian tribes in both Americas. The oldest ears of popcorn that have been found were in the Bat Cave in New Mexico. They have now been identified by radio-carbon tests to be about 5,600 years old.

Columbus discovered the natives in the West Indies wearing popcorn decorations like corsages. When Cortez invaded Mexico he found popcorn was an important food for the Aztec Indians. They also used it to decorate ceremonial headdresses, as necklaces and to ornament statues of their gods.

The English colonists were introduced to popcorn at the first Thanksgiving Feast at Plymouth, Massachusetts. The feast was actually a breakfast and ended with a surprise when a brave named Quadequina, brother of the Iro-

1

quois Chief, Massasoit, disappeared into the woods and returned with a deer-skin bag of popped popcorn as a gift. The Indians also brought popcorn "snacks" to meetings with the colonists as a token of goodwill. Those practical Colonial housewives put popcorn to mealtime use and served it with sugar and cream for breakfast—the first "puffed" cereal eaten by the white man.

Today, popcorn is a favorite food and the mainstay of the U.S. film industry. Its consumption has doubled in the last 10 years. We now eat more than 383,000,000 pounds of popcorn each year! Popcorn makers used to expand a kernal of popcorn 15 times its original size; now they puff a kernel to 40 times its size and even more. The product has been made more tender, the hull content reduced and even more than before, we are crazy about popcorn. And here is the big bonus: there is no need to feel guilty when you're eating it. Indian corn, including popcorn, of course, contains more food energy than 96% of all edible foods; it contains more protein when ripe than any other cereal grain; it provides the roughage needed in everyone's diet, and one cup of un-buttered popcorn contains only 54 calories! It is even often recommended as a between-meals snack by dentists because it contains no sugar. Naturally this doesn't apply to the glazed confections. Plain popcorn is a true whole grain cereal of great value, so pop it in good health.

This versatile native American food can be one of your best friends for good snacking, delicious confections and unusual decorations. You'll find excellent examples of each in this book.

3

WHAT MAKES IT POP?

Would you believe that a little demon lives inside each kernel and he becomes so angry when his "house" is heated that he throws a tantrum and causes it to burst? The Indian aborigines believed it.

If you prefer logic over imagination, modern science has another story. They say the moisture content of the kernels is the real reason for the pop. When the corn is heated, the moisture in the soft center of the kernel expands into steam. The hard starch outside of the kernel resists this steam until it builds up enough pressure and power to explode.

Take your pick.

POPCORN PATHOS

Back in the mid west, old-timers tell of a particular summer when it got so hot, the corn in the fields started popping right off the stalks. The cows and pigs thought it was a snow blizzard and they lay down and froze to death.

Have I ever lied to you before?

Storing Popcorn and Restoring The Pop

When you buy popcorn, check that the package is airtight and undamaged to be sure the kernels are at the proper moisture level for perfect popping.

Store your popcorn in a tightly covered plastic or glass container in a cool damp place. Your refrigerator is an ideal place to keep an opened package. Unopened packages can be stored in the freezer.

Different types and hybrids of popcorn pop differently. To find the one you like best you will simply have to experiment with the various brands.

If your popcorn has lost its zip and does not pop into fluffy, crisp kernels, it may have lost some of its important moisture. It can usually be restored by the following method:

Fill a 1 quart jar 3/4 full with popcorn and add 1 tablespoon water. Cover the jar tightly and shake vigorously and frequently, every five or ten minutes, until all the water is absorbed. Store in the refrigerator. In two to four days it should be ready for perfect popping.

Tips About Popcorn Poppers

Whether you use a heavy skillet over an open fire or an automatic corn popper, popcorn always seems to taste good. An electric popper is not necessary, but if you are going to buy one, here are some features to look for:

Look for the "Popcorn Institute Seal of Approval." This shows that the popper performed acceptably when tested under home conditions with institute supervision.

For general safety, look for:
   a. Heat-resistant handles on cover and unit.
   b. UL Approval (Underwriters' Laboratories) for both cord and unit.
   c. Securely fitting cover.

Some convenience features which make the job easier:
   a. Oil line for easy measuring
   b. Dishwasher-safe covers, unbreakable and see-through
   c. Easy-clean teflon surfaces

The design of the popper should provide for the escape of steam during the popping. Look for this feature. It keeps the popcorn from becoming soggy and reduces the chance of you getting spattered when the cover is removed. Steam escape features vary from popper to popper. Many have small vents around the cover; some are designed so that the cover fits into a ridge around the popper base with enough clearance for steam escape.

Know whether the popper you are considering is automatic or non-automatic. An automatic popper has a thermostat that shuts off the heating element at the end of the popping cycle. A non-automatic popper requires closer watching to prevent burning the popcorn once the cycle is complete. It must be promptly disconnected.

Additional features to look for that make for better popping:

a. The base of the popper should be curved or slanted. Flat-bottomed poppers can cause some of the kernels to scorch or burn because they will not circulate enough in the oil during popping.

b. As a general rule, poppers with higher wattages produce fluffier popcorn and better volume.

Popping Perfect Popcorn

One half cup corn equals about 4 quarts when popped. Wire poppers, used over coals will process about 1/4 cup popcorn at a time. A heavy lidded, or electric skillet, or 4 quart pressure pan will pop 1/2 cup corn at a time. Never overload your popper.

If you are operating an electric corn popper, follow the manufacturer's directions. If you have misplaced the directions (and who among us has not) these general directions will do nicely.

Warm the popper, heavy pan, or heavy skillet. Put in cooking oil, 3 table-spoons for a 3 quart popper, 1/4 cup oil for a 4 quart popper. Butter will not do because it will smoke or burn at the temperature necessary for good popping. Let the oil get hot—about three minutes. Drop in several kernels. When they begin to spin in the hot oil, it is time to start popping. Pour in enough kernels to cover the bottom of the pan, about 1/2 to 2/3 cup. A little shake before you start popping will make sure all the kernels are in contact with the oil. Cover, and if you are popping on top of the range rather than in a popper, shake gently over heat. When you hear the last few pops, remove pan from heat and empty contents into a large bowl.

For some interesting seasoning to pour over, see Special Popcorn Recipes, beginning on page 11.

CAMPFIRE POPPING

You can pop corn right on the grill or on the coals. In 12 inch squares of heavy-duty foil, put 1 teaspoon of oil and 1 tablespoon unpopped popcorn. Twist the ends to seal the packets loosely. Place the packets on hot coals or grill and listen to them pop! When the popping stops, remove the packets from the grill and open the tops. Season with melted butter and one of the good ideas you'll find in Special Popcorn Recipes, beginning on page 11.

Special Popcorn Recipes

Whether you are an impromptu party giver or a stay-at-home TV watcher popcorn is a friend. Inexpensive, delicious and versatile, it is small wonder more people are eating popcorn than ever before.

Not the least of popcorn's appeal is how easy and fast it is to prepare. You can even pop the corn earlier in the day, then warm it later. When you are ready to season and serve, simply spread the popped corn in a large roaster pan and warm in a low oven 250° for fifteen or twenty minutes.

When it comes to popcorn people love to improvise. Present a large bowlful of popped popcorn to even the most timid soul in any age group, and chances are he or she will come up with an interesting idea to season and flavor it.

If your imagination needs a nudge, we have some suggestions. Freshly popped and plain may be a reliable standby, but here are some new ways to drizzle, sprinkle and season your popcorn.

SEASONED POPCORNS — MORE THAN JUST BUTTER

There's alot more to popcorn than melted butter! Have you tried:

Blue Cheese Popcorn — Melt 1 cup butter. Stir in 1 package blue cheese salad dressing mix. Toss with 6 quarts freshly popped popcorn.

Parmesan Popcorn — Melt 1/4 cup butter. Pour over 2 quarts popped popcorn. Add 1/2 cup grated Parmesan cheese and 1/2 teaspoon salt. Mix well.

Sauteed Onion Popcorn — Saute 1/4 cup minced onion in 3 tablespoons butter until golden. Add 1/2 teaspoon salt. Toss with 2 quarts popcorn.

Curry Seasoned Popcorn — Melt 3 tablespoons butter in a small saucepan. Stir in 1/2 teaspoon salt, 1 teaspoon curry powder, 1/4 teaspoon ground cinnamon and 1/4 teaspoon ground ginger. Toss with 2 quarts popped popcorn.

Chili Seasoned Popcorn — Melt 3 tablespoons butter in small saucepan. Stir in 1 teaspoon chili powder, 1/2 teaspoon salt and 1/2 teaspoon paprika. Add to 2 quarts freshly popped popcorn. Toss well.

Herb Seasoned Popcorn — Melt 3 tablespoons butter in a small saucepan. Stir in 1/2 teaspoon salt. Crush 1 teaspoon thyme leaves, 1/2 teaspoon sweet basil leaves, 1/2 teaspoon oregano leaves and 1/2 teaspoon rosemary leaves. Add to butter. Pour over 2 quarts freshly popped popcorn. Toss well.

POPCORN FOR SEASONED SNACKERS

Make your own seasoned salt for this tangy popcorn.

3 qts. unsalted popped popcorn
1/2 cup melted butter
3 tbs. Seasoned Salt

Heat popcorn in a 250°F oven if it has been popped earlier. Pour melted butter over popcorn, tossing to mix. Sprinkle with seasoned salt and continue to toss until well mixed.

Seasoned Salt

6 tbs. salt	1/2 tsp. garlic salt	1/2 tsp. marjoram
2 tsp. paprika	1/2 tsp. celery salt	1/2 tsp. curry powder
1 tsp. dry mustard	1/2 tsp. thyme	1/2 tsp. dill weed

Combine all seasonings in a blender, or stir until well mixed.

POPCORN SNACKS THAT MAKE SENSE

When you're looking forward to a cozy afternoon of spectator sports in front of the TV, plan a snack with pizzazz but low on calories. Just sprinkle plain, freshly popped, warm popcorn with one or more of these:

garlic salt
curry powder
celery salt
chili powder
grated American cheese
grated Swiss cheese
parmesan cheese
French dressing
barbecue sauce
worcestershire sauce
nut meats
sesame seed
poppy seed

dried Italian herbs
hickory-flavored salt
vegetable flakes
butter-flavored salt
dry soup mix
dry dip mix
dill weed
bacon-flavored bits
canned onion rings
raisins
seasoned salt
powdered orange rind

POPCORN PARTY MIX

If you make this ahead, do warm it in a low oven for peak flavor.

3/4 cup (1-1/2 sticks) butter
1/2 tsp. garlic salt
1/2 tsp. onion salt
1/4 tsp. celery salt
1-1/2 tbs. Worcestershire sauce
1/8 tsp. Tabasco
3 qts. popped popcorn
1 cup pretzel sticks, broken
1-1/2 cups salted mixed nuts

Combine first six ingredients. Combine popcorn, pretzel pieces and nuts. Spread in a large roasting pan. Pour melted butter mixture over top and toss well to mix. Bake in a slow 275°F oven 1 hour, stirring 4 or 5 times. Makes about 3-1/2 quarts.

BACON-CHEESE POPCORN

4 qts. popped popcorn
1/3 cup butter, melted
1/2 tsp. seasoned salt
1/2 tsp. hickory-smoked salt
1/3 cup grated Parmesan cheese
1/3 cup bacon-flavored vegetable chips

Put freshly popped popcorn into a large bowl. Combine butter with seasoned and hickory-smoked salts. Pour over corn. Toss well to coat evenly. Sprinkle with cheese and bacon chips. Toss again and serve while warm. Makes 4 quarts.

MIX 'N MUNCH POPCORN

3 qts. unsalted popped popcorn
1/4 cup butter, melted
1/2 can (3-1/2 oz.) French fried onions
1/4 cup bacon bits or bacon flavored bits
salt

Toss popped corn with melted butter. Stir in French fried onions and bacon bits. Sprinkle with salt. Place mixture on a jelly roll pan or baking sheet. Heat in 250°F oven a few minutes. Serve hot. Makes 3 quarts.

PIZZA-PLEASER POPCORN

5 qts. unsalted popped popcorn
1/2 lb. pepperoni sausage, thinly sliced
1/4 cup (1/2 stick) butter
1/2 tsp. ground oregano
1/2 tsp. salt
2 tbs. grated Parmesan cheese

18

     Keep popcorn warm in a 200°F oven. Fry pepperoni till crisp. Drain on paper towels. Melt butter. Stir in oregano and salt. Combine popcorn and drained pepperoni. Pour seasoned butter over popcorn mixture. Toss well. Sprinkle with cheese. Makes 5 quarts.

CHILI CORN

A spicy cocktail nibble to offer your guests.

4 qts. popped popcorn
3 small dried red chilies
1 pkg. (6-3/4 oz.) peanuts
6 tbs. margarine
1 pkg. (3-1/4 oz.) roasted pepitas or sunflower seeds
3/4 tsp. garlic salt

Heat popped corn in oven if it is cold. Cook chilies and peanuts in margarine over low heat for 5 minutes. Remove chilies. Add pepitas and pour over hot corn; season with garlic salt.

POPCORN AND PEANUTS OLE

1 cup (4 ozs.) grated cheddar cheese
1 tbs. chili powder
1-1/2 tsp. ground cumin
1/2 tsp. ground coriander
1/4 tsp. celery salt
1/8 tsp. onion salt
1/8 tsp. garlic powder
few drops Tabasco
1 tsp. salt
1/8 tsp. cayenne pepper
3 qts. popped popcorn
1 cup cocktail peanuts

In a large bowl mix together the first ten ingredients. Add popcorn and peanuts to the mixture and thoroughly toss. Spread mixture on a 15-1/2 x 10-1/2 x 1 inch baking pan. Heat in a 350°F oven 8 to 10 minutes, stirring once. Makes about 12 cups.

BEEFY POPCORN

A satisfying snack! Because dried beef is salty don't add salt until you've tasted.

1 jar (2-1/2 ozs.) dried beef, chopped
1/2 cup butter
3 qts. unsalted popped popcorn

Cook dried beef in butter about 3 minutes. Heat popped popcorn in a 250°F oven if it has been popped earlier. Pour beef and butter over the popcorn. Toss to mix. Serve immediately. Makes 3 quarts.

SMOKY SKILLET POPCORN

Use a heavy skillet here, not your electric popper. Five or six pork sausage links may be sliced and used in place of the bacon.

3 to 4 slices bacon
1/2 cup popping corn
smoky flavored salt

Cube bacon and place in heavy 12 inch skillet over medium-high heat. (Or on a grill over campfire coals.) Cook, stirring until bacon fat cooks out enough to coat bottom of skillet. Add popping corn. Stir to mix well. Cover skillet loosely so that some steam can escape. Shake skillet back and forth until corn starts popping. Continue to shake skillet until popping slows down. Remove from heat or to edge of grill until corn finishes popping. Season with smoky flavored salt to taste. Makes about 4 quarts.

SOUP AND SALAD POPCORN PICKUPS

Here's a surprising garnish for tomato or cream soups, or for adding to tossed salads instead of croutons.

1 qt. unsalted popped popcorn
2 to 3 tbs. melted butter
1 tbs. charcoal salt, <u>or</u>
   1 tbs. garlic <u>or</u> onion salt, <u>or</u>
   1 tbs. dill weed <u>and</u> 1/2 tsp. salt

Heat popcorn in 250°F oven if it has been popped earlier. Pour melted butter over popcorn, tossing well to mix. Continue to toss and sprinkle with your choice of seasoning. Makes 1 quart.

POPCORN PACK-EATS

A novel way to end an outdoor barbecue. You assemble the ingredients and the foil and let each guest make his own creation.

unsalted popped popcorn
squares of heavy duty foil
Assortment of: semi-sweet chocolate or butterscotch morsels,
   milk chocolate bars (broken into squares) or kisses
   miniature marshmallows
   crushed peppermint candy
   salted pecans or peanuts

For each Pack-Eat, put popcorn in the center of a foil square. Each person tops the popcorn with his own favorite "eats." Bring foil up over popcorn and fold top and ends to make a packet. Place packet on grill over ashen-gray charcoal coals until heated through, about 10 mintues. Turn once. To eat, open packet and push back foil.

CHOCOLATE POPCORN AND PEANUTS

2 tbs. butter or margarine
1 pkg. (6 ozs.) semi-sweet chocolate pieces
12 large marshmallows
1 tbs. water
2 qts. popped popcorn
1 cup cocktail peanuts

26

Melt butter in large saucepan over low heat. Add chocolate pieces, marshmallows and water. Stir constantly until chocolate and marshmallows are melted and mixture is smooth. Add popcorn and toss until well coated. Add peanuts and toss. Spread out in a shallow pan to cool. Makes about 2 quarts.

CHOCOLATE MINT POPCORN

1/4 cup butter
4 to 6 chocolate-covered mint patties, broken into pieces
2 qts. popped popcorn, more or less

Melt butter and patties in heavy saucepan over low heat. Pour over popcorn, about 2 quarts, depending on how thick you like your chocolate.

CHOCO-O-SCOTCH NIBBLERS

1 pkg. (6 ozs.) semi-sweet chocolate pieces
1 pkg. (6 ozs.) butterscotch pieces
1 pkg. (6-1/4 ozs.) miniature marshmallows
1 qt. buttered and salted popped popcorn
mixed nuts, if desired

Toss ingredients together in a large bowl. Makes about 2 quarts.

EASY PARTY POPCORN

Sweet treats for children's parties . . . so much less expensive than candy and without the trouble of making a syrup. Each makes three quarts.

2 cups miniature marshmallows
1/2 cup melted butter

3 qts. unsalted popped popcorn
1 pkg. (3 ozs.) fruit-flavored gelatin

Combine marshmallows and butter. Pour over popped popcorn and mix well. Sprinkle gelatin over all and toss to mix well.

CINNAMON-SUGAR POPCORN

1/2 cup sugar
1 tbs. cinnamon

1/2 cup melted butter
3 qts. unsalted popped popcorn

Combine sugar and cinnamon. Pour melted butter over popcorn, tossing as you pour. Sprinkle with cinnamon-sugar. Toss until well mixed.

LADY-LIKE POPCORN

A less sweet, lighter confection.

1/4 cup butter, melted
5 qts. popped popcorn
4 tsp. grated lemon peel
1/4 cup sugar
1/4 tsp. mace

Pour melted butter over popped popcorn. Spread buttered popcorn on baking sheet. Combine grated lemon peel, sugar and mace. Sprinkle over buttered popcorn. Place in 325°F oven 3 to 5 minutes. Makes 5 quarts.

BAKED POPCORN CRUNCH

A delicious company treat to serve with cocoa, spiced tea, or cola drinks. Try it the next time the meeting is at your house.

1/2 cup butter
1/2 cup brown sugar
3 qts. unsalted popped popcorn
1 cup whole pecans or mixed nuts

Cream butter. Add brown sugar and cream until fluffy. Mix popcorn and pecans together. Combine with creamed mixture. Spread in a long baking pan. Bake in a 350°F oven about 8 minutes or until crisp. Makes about 3 quarts.

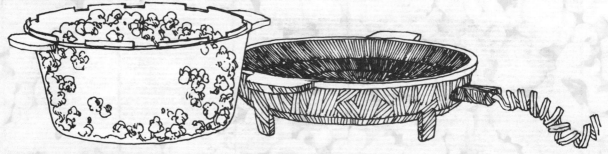

POPCORN COOKIES

Here's an unusual way to use popcorn! You'll like the flavor it gives these light, delicate cookies.

3 cups popped popcorn	2/3 cup sugar
2 tbs. butter, softened	1/2 tsp. salt
2 egg whites	1 tsp. vanilla

Place popcorn, 1 cup at a time, in an electric blender container. Cover and blend until finely ground. Turn out into quart measuring cup. Continue until you have 1-1/2 cups ground popcorn. Stir ground popcorn and butter together. Beat egg whites on high speed until stiff. Gradually add sugar, beating on low speed after each addition, until mixture is stiff and glossy. Beat in salt and vanilla. Fold in popcorn mixture. Drop by heaping teaspoonfuls onto greased baking sheets about 3 inches apart. Bake in 325°F oven 12 to 15 minutes or until firm and lightly browned. Remove from baking sheets at once. Makes 30 cookies.

Glazed Popcorn Confections

Popcorn has been a part of Christmas since the Indians taught the Pilgrims how to plant and cook corn. In some kitchens the aroma of popcorn mingled with that of a sweet syrup means the family is making popcorn balls. But there are dozens of other treats to make and enjoy the year round and all from the same easy steps:

Pop some popcorn

Boil up a flavored syrup

Toss the two together and mold it, color it, break it into chunks, decorate it, or just EAT IT. When you learn how to make and test the syrup and to toss it correctly over the popcorn, you have learned the whole secret of a delightful activity and good eating, too.

Cheaper than ice cream, less fattening than candy, popcorn is the oldest truly American confection.

TESTING THE SYRUP

When water and sugar are boiled together, they form a syrup. The longer they boil, the thicker the syrup becomes. Some recipes will tell you what degree on a candy thermometer should be reached. More frequently, a recipe will require a degree of firmness called soft ball, firm ball or crack stage.

To test the syrup, fill a china or glass cup half full of water. Drop about 1/4 teaspoon of the syrup into the water and work it together with your fingers, into a ball.

<u>Soft ball stage</u> — syrup will hold together in a round ball but will gradually lose its shape when removed from the cool water and placed on a flat surface.

<u>Firm ball stage</u> — syrup will hold together in a firm ball which clicks slightly and will not stick when it is tapped against the side of the cup. It will retain its shape when removed from the cool water and placed on a flat surface.

<u>Crack stage</u> — syrup will separate into threads when it hits the cool water. It will be too stiff to form into a smooth ball.

MIXING THE SYRUP WITH THE POPCORN

You will need a container such as a roasting pan or canning kettle with high sides and large enough so the popcorn takes up no more than 1/3 of the space. If you rinse the container with hot water, dry it well and then generously rub it with soft margarine, you will be glad you did. Less sticking and easier mixing result in a warm, buttered container.

Butter two long wooden spoons almost to the end of each handle.

Be careful, that syrup will be hot! Protect your hands while shaping the popcorn with a pair of clean, dampened, cotton gloves.

To work more quickly and to share the fun, invite a helper or two.

If the popcorn was popped earlier, warm it in a slow 250° oven while the syrup cooks. The syrup mixes easier through warm popcorn.

Pour cooked syrup over the warm popcorn while your helper gives the bowl quarter turns. Using both spoons toss the popcorn like a salad until evenly coated, at least 200 strokes.

Now, the glazed popcorn is ready to be shaped or simply spread out to cool. Butter your hands if popcorn has cooled, or wear dampened gloves.

THREE SYRUPS FOR POPCORN CONFECTIONS

Here are three basic and delicious syrups to make and pour over popcorn for eating and decorating. If a candy thermometer is not available test the syrup according to instructions on page 34. <u>Each of these syrups will flavor 6 cups of popped popcorn</u>. Combine syrup and hot popcorn as directed on the preceding pages. Shape or use as desired.

Caramel Syrup

1-1/2 tbs. butter
1-1/2 cups brown sugar
6 tbs. water

Combine ingredients in heavy saucepan. Stir over medium heat until sugar is dissolved. Bring to a boil. Cover and cook about 3 minutes until the steam has washed down the sides of pan. Uncover and cook without stirring to the soft-ball stage, 238°.

Molasses Syrup

1 tbs. butter   1/2 cup molasses   1/4 cup sugar

Combine ingredients in a saucepan. Stir over medium heat until sugar is dissolved. Bring to a boil. Cover and cook about 3 minutes until steam has washed down sides of pan. Uncover and cook, without stirring, nearly to the hard-crack stage, 290°.

White Sugar Syrup – Add a flavoring and tint with food coloring.

2/3 cup sugar   2-1/2 tbs. white corn syrup   1/3 tsp. vinegar
1/2 cup water   1/8 tsp. salt

Combine ingredients in saucepan. Stir until sugar is dissolved. Bring to a boil. Cook covered 3 minutes until steam washes down sides of pan. Uncover and cook, without stirring, nearly to the hard-crack stage, 290°.

CARAMEL CORN

Here are two ways to make that old favorite, Caramel Corn, plus some delicious variations on how to use it.

Old Fashioned Caramel Corn

3 qts. popped popcorn
1-1/2 cups granulated sugar
3/4 cup dark corn syrup

3/4 cup water
3 tbs. butter
2 tsp. vinegar

Keep popcorn warm in a low 200°F oven while you make the syrup. Measure remaining ingredients in a 3 quart saucepan. Stir mixture over low heat until sugar is dissolved. Cook, without stirring, to 270° on a candy thermometer. Place warm popcorn in a greased bowl. Pour syrup over popcorn. Stir as you pour to coat every kernel. Spread on greased surface to cool.

Peanut Crunch — Add 1/2 pound salted peanuts to the popcorn while it is being mixed with the syrup.

Super Easy Caramel Corn

3 qts. popped popcorn   2 tbs. water
1 lb. caramels

Keep popcorn warm in a low 200°F oven. Melt caramels with water in the top of a double boiler over hot water. Place warm popcorn in a greased bowl. Pour caramel syrup over popcorn. Stir well to mix. Spread on a greased surface to cool and set. Break apart and serve.

Variations

Caramel Corn Ice Cream Balls — Roll ice cream balls into chopped caramel corn. Serve at once or freeze until firm then wrap in foil and store in freezer.

Caramel Corn Cake — Double caramel corn recipe. Press into a buttered angel food cake pan. Cool, then loosen edges and invert pan. For "frosting" melt 1 pound caramels with 2 tablespoons water. Drizzle over cake.

BAKED CARAMEL CORN

A man who "knows his popcorn" says this is the best caramel corn in the whole world.

1 cup (1/2 lb.) butter or margarine
2 cups firmly packed brown sugar
1/2 cup light or dark corn syrup
1 tsp. salt
1/2 tsp. baking soda
1 tsp. vanilla
6 qts. popped popcorn

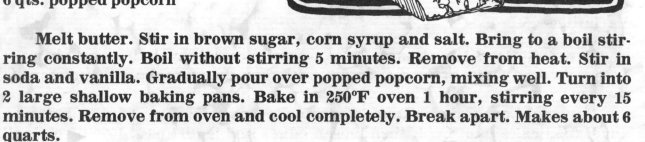

Melt butter. Stir in brown sugar, corn syrup and salt. Bring to a boil stirring constantly. Boil without stirring 5 minutes. Remove from heat. Stir in soda and vanilla. Gradually pour over popped popcorn, mixing well. Turn into 2 large shallow baking pans. Bake in 250°F oven 1 hour, stirring every 15 minutes. Remove from oven and cool completely. Break apart. Makes about 6 quarts.

CARAMEL CORN CLUSTERS

This syrup cooks quickly and doesn't require testing or a candy thermometer . . . very easy for something so tasty.

28 caramels
1/4 cup sugar
1/4 cup water
2 qts. popped popcorn
1 cup peanuts

Combine caramels, sugar and water in saucepan. Cook over low heat, stirring constantly, until mixture is smooth and comes to a full boil. Continue to stir constantly while mixture boils gently for 5 minutes. Combine popcorn and peanuts in large baking pan. Pour caramel syrup over popcorn mixture. Toss quickly with two buttered forks until popcorn and peanuts are well coated. Spread mixture on cookie sheets. Let stand until cold, then break into clusters.

CARMEL CORN BRITTLE

A peanut and popcorn combination you'll find hard to stop eating.

2 qts. popped popcorn
1/2 cup dry roasted peanuts
1 cup sugar
1/2 cup corn syrup
1/2 water

2 tbs. molasses
2 tbs. butter
1 tsp. vinegar
1 tsp. baking soda

42

Combine popcorn and nuts in a buttered 9 x 13 x 2 inch pan. In a heavy saucepan, combine sugar, syrup, water, molasses, butter and vinegar. Stir mixture while heating until sugar dissolves. Cook over medium heat, without stirring, until mixture reaches 300° or hard crack stage. Remove from heat. Add baking soda, quickly stirring only enough to mix. Pour over popcorn and nuts and toss well to coat. Turn mixture out on a large buttered surface. With two forks, pull apart into pieces as thin as possible. Let cool and break into smaller pieces.

APPLE POPCORN BRITTLE

1 qt. popped popcorn
2 cups apple and cinnamon flavored cereal
1 cup cocktail peanuts
3/4 cup apple juice
1 cup sugar
1/4 cup light corn syrup
1/2 tsp. vinegar
1/4 tsp. salt

In a bowl, toss together popped popcorn, cereal and peanuts. Set aside. Butter sides of a heavy 2 quart saucepan. In saucepan combine apple juice, sugar, corn syrup, vinegar and salt. Cook over medium heat, stirring constantly until sugar dissolves and mixture begins to boil. Cook to the hard ball stage (250° on a candy thermometer). Remove from heat. Pour syrup over popcorn-cereal-peanut mixture. Toss well to coat. Spread in a buttered 15-1/2 x 10-1/2 x 1 inch baking pan. Cool until hardened. Break into pieces.

MOTHER NATURE'S MUNCH

What is more wholesome than peanuts, popcorn, wheat germ and raisins? This is a combination you owe it to the snackers in your house to try.

2 qts. popped popcorn
1 cup cocktail peanuts
1 cup wheat germ
1 cup seedless raisins
1/4 cup butter

1 cup sugar
1/3 cup honey
1/3 cup water
1/2 tsp. salt

Toss together the popcorn, peanuts, wheat germ and raisins. Set aside. In a buttered 2 quart saucepan melt butter. Stir in sugar, honey, water and salt. Cook over medium heat, stirring constantly, until sugar is dissolved and mixture begins to boil. Continue cooking until mixture reaches 250° on a candy thermometer or the hard ball stage. Pour slowly over popcorn/peanut mixture. Stir to coat. Spread into two buttered 15-1/2 x 10-1/2 x 1 inch baking pans. Bake in a preheated 250°F oven 45 minutes, stirring every 10 or 15 minutes. Makes about 10 cups.

JOLLY KA-RUNCH!

2 qts. popped popcorn
1 cup peanuts
1 cup almonds
1-1/3 cups sugar
1 cup margarine or butter
1 tsp. vanilla
1/2 cup white corn syrup
1/2 tsp. cream of tartar
1/2 tsp. soda

46

Mix popcorn and nuts together in large container. Combine sugar, butter, vanilla and corn syrup in saucepan. Cook over medium heat to the hard ball stage. Syrup is ready when a small amount makes a firm ball in cold water. Cooking time is short, about 5 minutes. Remove from heat. Add soda, then vanilla. Pour over popcorn and nuts. Mix to coat well. Spread out on cookie sheets to cool and dry. When cold break apart and store in tightly covered container. Makes about 2 pounds.

POPCORN CHRISTMAS CRUNCH

1 cup butter
1 cup sugar
2 tbs. water
1 tbs. light corn syrup
3 cups popped popcorn
1/2 cup natural cereal

Melt butter in a heavy 3 quart saucepan over low heat. Remove saucepan from heat and blend in sugar. Return to low heat, stirring constantly, until mixture reaches a full boil. Stir in water and corn syrup. Continue stirring and cooking over low heat until mixture reaches 270° or the soft crack stage on a candy thermometer. Remove from heat and stir in popcorn. Spread mixture in a buttered 15-1/2 x 10-1/2 x 1 inch baking pan. Immediately sprinkle with natural cereal. Cool until hardened and break into large pieces, as with peanut brittle. Makes approximately one pound.

QUICK MOLASSES POPCORN BALLS

3 qts. popped popcorn
1 cup mild molasses*
1 cup sugar
1/2 tsp. salt
1 tsp. vanilla

    Keep popcorn warm in a 200°F oven. Combine molasses, sugar and salt in a 2-quart saucepan. Cook over medium heat, stirring constantly, until mixture comes to a boil. Cook without stirring 4 minutes. Remove from heat. Stir in vanilla. Pour syrup over popcorn slowly. Toss and mix to distribute syrup evenly. When cool enough to handle but still quite warm, shape into balls. Let stand until cool and no longer sticky. Wrap in plastic film or put each ball in a small plastic bag and tie securely. Store in tightly covered container. Makes about 10 medium popcorn balls.

*For a milder molasses flavor, use 1/2 cup molasses and 1/2 cup corn syrup.

HONEYED POPCORN BALLS

These balls are not only good—they combine two energy-making foods besides.

3 qts. slightly salted popcorn
3/4 cup honey
1-1/4 cups light corn syrup
1 tbs. butter
1/2 tbs. vinegar
1 tsp. salt
1/2 tsp. vanilla

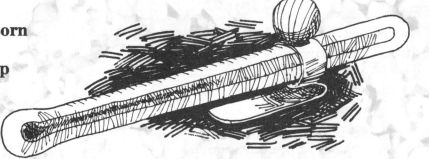

In a 2 quart saucepan boil the honey, syrup, butter, vinegar and salt. Stir mixture frequently until it reaches 275°F on a candy thermometer. Remove from heat. Add vanilla. Pour over popcorn and stir to coat. With buttered hands form into balls.

PURPLE POPCORN BALLS —
OR GREEN, OR ORANGE, OR YELLOW, OR . . .

Popcorn balls with pizazz!

2 cups sugar
1 can (6 ozs.) frozen fruit juice concentrate — grape, orange,
    limeade,lemonade, etc.
1 can (6 ozs.) water
1/2 cup light corn syrup
1 tsp. vinegar
1/2 tsp. salt
5 qts. unsalted popped popcorn

Combine all ingredients, except popcorn, in a heavy saucepan. Bring to a boil. Lower heat and cook to 250° on a candy thermometer or hard ball stage. Mixture will bubble up in pan, so watch carefully to keep it from boiling over. Pour slowly onto hot popcorn and mix until well coated. Let stand 5 minutes or until mixture can be easily formed into balls. Butter hands and form into 3 inch balls. Makes about 18 balls.

PEPPERMINT POPCORN LOLLIPOPS

Room-mothers take note . . . these always make a big hit at classroom parties.

6 qts. popped popcorn
1 lb. peppermint stick candy, crushed
2 lbs. marshmallows
1/2 cup butter or margarine
small peppermint sticks

Combine popcorn and crushed peppermint in a large container. Melt butter and marshmallows in large saucepan over low heat. Pour over popcorn mixture. Mix well. Wet hands and shape into balls. Lay on waxed paper. Insert a peppermint stick in each ball. Makes about 24 small balls.

ORANGE POPCORN CLOWNS

Little hands like making the clowns and decorating their faces.

6 qts. popped popcorn
3-1/2 cups sugar
1 cup light corn syrup
1 cup orange juice
grated peel from 2 oranges

1/2 tsp. salt
4 to 6 drops orange coloring
1/4 cup butter
12 pointed ice cream cones
gum drops for decorating

Keep popcorn warm in a 200°F oven. Cook sugar, corn syrup, orange juice, peel and salt in heavy saucepan to the firm ball stage (246°). Remove from heat and stir in butter and food coloring. Pour over warm popcorn. Toss to coat well. Working with wet hands fill cones with candied popcorn, rounding tops like big scoops of ice cream. Turn cones upside down on waxed paper. Set at angle so clown's hat is slightly tipped. Press to flatten bottom so clown won't fall over. Decorate with gumdrops for eyes, noses, mouths and pom poms. Makes 12 clowns.

HALLOWEEN POPCORN BALLS

The magic of candy corn turns an old favorite into a Halloween treat. Pile in your biggest bowl for an edible party decoration.

5 qts. popped popcorn
1 cup candy corn
4 tbs. butter
1 cup packed brown sugar
1/2 cup light corn syrup
2/3 cup sweetened condensed milk (not evaporated)
1/2 tsp. vanilla

Mix together popcorn and candy corn. Set aside. Melt butter in a 2 quart saucepan. Stir in sugar and syrup. Bring to boiling over medium heat. Stir in condensed milk. Boil gently, stirring constantly, until mixture reaches the soft ball stage 234°, about 15 to 20 minutes. Stir in vanilla. Pour over popcorn mixture. Stir to coat well. Butter hands lightly. Shape into popcorn balls about 2 inches in diameter. Makes about 20 popcorn balls.

PEANUT BUTTER POPCORN BALLS

And who doesn't like peanut butter? These are good plain, topped with chocolate (page 56) or made into surprise balls with M & M peanut candies hidden in the center.

4 qts. (16 cups) popped popcorn
1-1/2 cups sugar
1-1/2 cups light corn syrup
1-1/2 cups peanut butter
1-1/2 tsp. vanilla

Keep popcorn warm in a slow 200°F oven. Mix sugar and corn syrup together in heavy saucepan. Bring to a full boil. Boil 30 seconds, stirring constantly. Remove from heat and beat in peanut butter and vanilla. Pour syrup over popcorn. Stir quickly to mix well. Shape into 16 balls.

CHOCOLATE TOPPED MOCHA BALLS

3 qts. popped popcorn
2/3 cup sugar
1/2 cup water
2 tbs. instant coffee
2-1/2 tbs. white corn syrup
1/8 tsp. salt
1/2 tsp. vinegar
1 tsp. vanilla
1 pkg. (6 ozs.) semi-sweet chocolate pieces

56

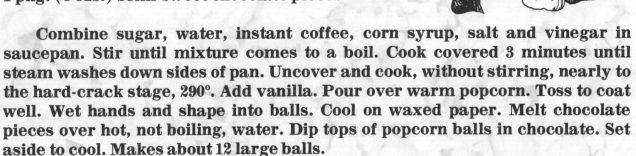

Combine sugar, water, instant coffee, corn syrup, salt and vinegar in saucepan. Stir until mixture comes to a boil. Cook covered 3 minutes until steam washes down sides of pan. Uncover and cook, without stirring, nearly to the hard-crack stage, 290°. Add vanilla. Pour over warm popcorn. Toss to coat well. Wet hands and shape into balls. Cool on waxed paper. Melt chocolate pieces over hot, not boiling, water. Dip tops of popcorn balls in chocolate. Set aside to cool. Makes about 12 large balls.

CRANBERRY POPCORN BALLS

A spicy, attractive addition to your holiday treats.

1-1/2 cups water
1 tsp. whole cloves
1 tsp. whole allspice
2 sticks cinnamon
1 cup chopped cranberries
1-1/3 cups sugar

2 tbs. light corn syrup
1 tbs. shredded orange peel
1/4 tsp. ground nutmeg
3 to 4 drops red food coloring
12 cups popped popcorn

Pour water into a buttered 2 quart saucepan. Tie cloves, allspice and cinnamon in a piece of cheesecloth. Add to water. Cover and simmer 20 minutes. Remove spices from pan. Stir in cranberries, sugar, corn syrup, orange peel, nutmeg and food coloring. Cook over medium heat, stirring constantly until sugar is dissolved and mixture begins to boil. Cook without stirring until mixture reaches hard-ball stage, 250°. Pour syrup over popcorn, stirring well to coat. Lightly butter hands and shape into balls. Makes about 12 balls.

PEANUTTY CHOCO-POP BARS

1/2 cup butter
1 cup firmly packed light brown sugar
1/4 cup each light corn syrup and water
1 tsp. salt
2-1/2 qts. popped popcorn
1 bar (7.3 ozs.) milk chocolate
1 cup chunky peanut butter
cocktail peanuts

Melt butter in a 2 quart saucepan. Stir in sugar, syrup, water and salt. Cook over medium heat, stirring constantly until sugar is dissolved and mixture begins to boil. Cook until mixture reaches the hard ball stage (250°). Place popcorn in a large bowl. Pour caramel mixture over popcorn, stirring to coat. Press coated popcorn into a buttered 15-1/2 x 10-1/2 x 1 inch baking pan. Heat chocolate and peanut butter together over low heat until chocolate is melted. Spread evenly over caramel popcorn. Cool until topping is set. Cut into bars and garnish with whole peanuts. Makes about 49 3 x 1-1/2 inch bars.

CANDY-TOPPED POPCORN BARS

Be sure to use as many different colored candies as possible and press them into the popcorn mixture while it is warm and soft.

3 qts. popped popcorn
1 cup sugar
1/3 cup light corn syrup
1/3 cup water

1/4 cup butter or margarine
3/4 tsp. salt
3/4 tsp. vanilla
Lifesaver candies

Keep popcorn warm in slow 200°F oven. Combine sugar, syrup, water, butter and salt in saucepan. Stir over medium heat until sugar dissolves. Continue cooking, without stirring, until mixture forms a brittle ball (270°) in cold water. Add vanilla and stir only enough to mix it through the hot syrup. Place popcorn in large container and slowly pour syrup over top. Mix quickly and well until every kernel is coated. Wet hands slightly. Transfer mixture to well-buttered flat cake pan. Decorate with rows of Lifesavers pressed into top so they stand up. Cool popcorn then remove to a cutting board. Using a wet knife, cut between rows of candies and then into bars.

PARTY POPCORN CAKE

Here's the kind of cake that makes sense for small children's parties. It's sturdy, pretty, certainly less messy than the traditional kind, and "little ones" usually like it better!

8 qts. popped popcorn
1 pkg. (1 lb.) gumdrops, cut up (do not use black ones)
1/2 lb. butter or margarine
2 lbs. marshmallows

Combine popcorn and gumdrops in a large container. Melt butter and marshmallows in a large saucepan over low heat. Pour over popcorn and gumdrops. Mix well. Press mixture into a well buttered 10 inch tube pan. Cake is ready to slice and eat in 1 hour. It does not need to be refrigerated.

SOUTHERN POPCORN CAKE

My favorite Southern belle recommends this as the way they make popcorn cake in Kentucky.

4 qts. popped popcorn
1 cup broken nuts
1-1/2 tsp. salt
1 cup molasses
1 cup dark corn syrup
1 tbs. butter
candied cherries

Toss popcorn, nuts and salt in a large container. Combine molasses and syrup. Boil until a soft ball forms when a little syrup is dropped into cold water. Add butter. Pour gradually over salted popcorn and nuts. Mix well Pack firmly into greased 10 inch tube pan. Let stand 2 or 3 hours in pan. Remove cake from pan and garnish with cut cherries. Slice into wedges to serve.

POPCORN NUT SLICES

This great combination of flavors is ready to eat in little over an hour.

3 qts. popped popcorn
1/4 lb. butter or margarine
1 pkg. (6 ozs.) semi-sweet chocolate pieces
1 pkg. (10-1/2 ozs.) miniature marshmallows
2 cups Spanish peanuts
2 cups chopped pecans or almonds
1 half-gallon milk carton

62

Keep popcorn warm in slow 200°F oven. Melt butter, chocolate and marshmallows together in top of double boiler over hot, not boiling, water. Place popcorn in large container. Pour chocolate syrup over popcorn, adding nuts gradually as you toss mixture. Mix thoroughly until popcorn and nuts are well coated. Spoon mixture into milk carton, packing tightly. Place in refrigerator 1 hour. Cut carton lengthwise along all 4 corners and peel carton away. Slice and serve.

CHOCOLATE POPCORN PIE

Nobody says it can't be butterscotch or banana cream if you prefer.

2 qts. popped popcorn
White Sugar Syrup, page 37
1 pkg. (6 ozs.) chocolate pudding & pie filling
whipped cream

Keep popcorn warm in a low 200°F oven while making syrup. Place warm popcorn in large, buttered bowl. Drizzle syrup over popcorn. Stir until well coated. Press mixture into a 9 inch pie plate, building edges higher than the plate edge. Butter your fingers because they are sure to get into the molding process. Allow crust to cool. Prepare pudding according to package directions. Cover with plastic wrap pressed firmly against the surface to prevent a skin from forming. Chill thoroughly. When ready to serve spoon pudding into popcorn shell. Garnish with whipped cream. Makes 6 to 8 servings.

Parties and Decorations

Long before the time of Jesus or even Confucius, Indians were growing, popping, eating and even wearing popcorn. They knew the best use of the mysterious bursting corn was to eat it, but they always used it for decorative purposes too. Over 5000 years ago Mexican Indians were stringing popcorn for religious ceremonies. It was cultivated by the Incas and used to decorate bodies for burial. It has been a part of our Christmas decorations since the Indians shared their knowledge of popcorn with the white men.

The reminder here is — it is great any time of the year. Whenever you want to be different and deliciously decorative, use popcorn. Popcorn creations and centerpieces are fun for holidays, birthdays, showers and all your special occasions. Try a few ideas and your imagination will lead you to more of your own devising. When making your own creations, use any of the syrups in the section, Popcorn Confections. Also read how to test and toss the syrup.

One word of warning: when you are planning to decorate with popcorn, pop mountains of it. More always ends up in the stomach than anywhere else.

A BON VOYAGE PARTY

Treat some lucky friends (or yourself) to a happy cruise send-off. Send invitations to look like travel tickets or passports. Travel posters will set the scene and have popcorn leis for all your guests. Just string unseasoned popcorn on thread. Spray with vegetable coloring and let them dry. They will look festive and floral, but they will not be good for eating. For good nibbling offer your guests Vacation Island Crunch:

8 cups popped popcorn
1 cup salted pecans
2 cans (12 ozs. ea.) root beer
1 cup sugar
1/2 cup light corn syrup
1/2 cup butter or margarine
1/4 tsp. salt

Combine popcorn and pecans in a buttered bowl. Pour root beer slowly down side of heavy saucepan. Add sugar, syrup, butter and salt. Cook over medium heat. Bring to a boil, stirring until sugar melts. Cook to 290°F (hard crack stage). Pour in a fine stream over popcorn and pecans. Toss until popcorn is coated with syrup. Spread onto 2 buttered baking sheets and separate with a fork. Cool. Makes 12 cups.

POPCORN CARAMEL CRAZY DAISIES

When you are going all out for a girls-only, ever so dainty luncheon or party these popcorn daisies will give everyone a smile. Use them as place cards or for a centerpiece.

1 pkg. (14 ozs.) caramels
1/4 cup water
4 qts. popped popcorn, salted
wooden sticks
paper flower cutouts
toothpicks

68

Melt caramels with water in a saucepan over low heat. Stir until sauce is smooth. Pour over popcorn. Toss until well-coated. Moisten hands with cold water and shape popcorn into 12 balls. Insert a wooden stick in each. Cut from colored paper 12 petal-edged flowers that are 3 inches wider in diameter than the popcorn balls. Place a popcorn ball in the center of each flower and fasten with toothpicks. Use in a centerpiece cluster or at each place setting.

EASY PARTY IDEAS

Be sure to read section Glazed Popcorn Confections, page 33, for instructions on how to glaze and mold popcorn.

Line a jack-o-lantern with aluminum foil and fill it with your favorite popcorn, or Halloween Popcorn Balls, page 53.

Make a large popcorn ball and use in the center of an appetizer tray as a holder for hors d'oeuvres on toothpicks.

Instead of fortune cookies, try Popcorn Fortune Balls. Type up predictions or sayings and mold them inside popcorn balls.

Mold dainty popcorn dessert shells using turned-over buttered glass custard cups or small cereal dishes. Work quickly and don't forget that food coloring added to the cooked syrup will give a pretty pastel touch. Fill shells just before serving with sherbet, ice cream, fruit or pudding.

Popcorn Lollipops are inexpensive favors for a small-fry party. Glaze popped popcorn (caramel is delicious) and press into well buttered muffin tins. Stick in a skewer or popsicle stick. Gently remove the Lollipops from pans and place on waxed paper until set.

POPCORN BLOSSOM TREE

The perfect centerpiece for a spring table.

1 graceful but sturdy branch from a bush or tree, 10 to 12 inches long
1 block of wood to hold the branch
miniature paper parasols, tiny birds, dolls, whistles, kites or favors
3 qts. popped popcorn
1 lb. miniature marshmallows
1/4 cup butter
3 tbs. undissolved peach gelatin or
   3 drops orange food coloring

To assemble the tree drill a hole in the block of wood and insert the branch upright to resemble a growing tree. Set aside until needed. Keep popcorn warm in a 200°F oven while preparing the syrup. Measure marshmallows, butter and gelatin into the top of a double boiler over boiling water. Stir until marshmallows are melted and blended with gelatin. Place popcorn in a large

buttered pan. Pour syrup over the popcorn and mix well. (Read about mixing the syrup on page 35.) Attach small clusters of candied popcorn along the "tree" branches to resemble a tree in blossom. Allow to dry thoroughly. Complete the tree with the parasols or other small decorations tied on with ribbons. Place the tree on the table it is to decorate. Scatter a few clusters of candied popcorn around the base for fallen blossoms.

POPCORN GARDEN HAT

Here is a party centerpiece to please little or big girls. Use the light glaze that follows or make **White Sugar Syrup on page 37.**

2 cups sugar
1 cup light corn syrup
1 cup water
1/2 cup butter

2 qts. popped popcorn
small bowl
heavy duty foil
ribbon and flowers

Combine sugar, corn syrup, water and butter in saucepan. Cook to the hard-ball stage, 260°. If you wish, tint by adding a few drops of food coloring to the cooked syrup. Pour syrup over popcorn and mix thoroughly. Press a portion of the coated popcorn into a small, well-greased bowl to form crown of hat. Remove bowl immediately. Quickly press remaining coated popcorn onto a 10 inch circle drawn on a square of heavy duty foil. Lift foil at each corner to make ripples in the popcorn "brim." Allow to set a minute or two. Place crown in center of brim. Decorate with a ribbon band and fresh or artificial flowers. Tuck excess foil under hat.

CHERRY-FILLED POPCORN HEART

For a Valentine party this popcorn heart carries out the theme and color scheme while doubling as centerpiece and delicious dessert.

2 qts. unsalted popped popcorn
2 cups granulated sugar
1 cup light corn syrup
1 cup water
1/2 cup butter
1 No. 2 can (2-1/2 cups) cherry pie filling

Place popcorn in large buttered bowl. Draw a heart on a sheet of heavy-duty foil, approximately 8 inches in diameter. Combine sugar, syrup, water and butter in a saucepan and cook to 260° (soft crack stage). Pour syrup over popcorn and mix thoroughly. Quickly press onto foil heart, building up edges to form a rim. Allow to cool. Spoon cherry pie filling into heart-shaped popcorn shell. Serve with a dollop of ice cream. Makes 4 to 6 servings.

POPCORN DIZZY-DISKS

An easy-to-make decoration for a Halloween Party. You make the disks and let the children do the decorating.

2 qts. warm unsalted popped popcorn
2/3 cup light corn syrup
2/3 cup sugar
1 tsp. salt
food coloring
candies — lifesavers, black licorice strings, candy corn, jelly beans, gumdrops
chewing gum — chiclet-style miniatures
materials — construction paper, round-headed straight pins, ribbon, sequins

Keep popcorn hot and crisp in a 200°F oven. In a heavy, medium saucepan, combine corn syrup, sugar and salt. Bring to boiling over medium heat. Boil 2 minutes, stirring constantly. Add food coloring until desired color is obtained. Pour syrup slowly over popcorn and toss lightly to coat kernels evenly. (Read how to test and toss in Popcorn Confections, page 34.) Pack popcorn into 3 buttered, miniature layer cake pans (5 x 1 inches). Let cool. Twist popcorn disks to loosen and tap out of pans. Decorate each disk to resemble a Jack O'lantern, an owl, a witch, or other seasonal symbol. Or, with buttered hands, shape glazed popcorn quickly into 3 thick, flat 5 inch circles. You may also pack the popcorn into buttered, 3 inch egg-poaching rings.

POPCORN PILGRIMS

3/4 cup water
1 cup sugar
1/4 cup light corn syrup
1 pkg. (1/2 oz.) Kool Aid
1/2 tsp. vinegar

1/4 tsp. salt
1/2 tsp. vanilla
2-1/2 qts. popped popcorn
decorating materials*

Butter sides of a heavy 2 quart saucepan. Combine water, sugar, corn syrup, Kool Aid, vinegar and salt in saucepan. Cook over medium heat, stirring constantly, until sugar dissolves and mixture begins to boil. Continue cooking to 250° (hard ball stage). Remove saucepan from heat. Quickly stir vanilla into mixture. Pour over popcorn. Toss to coat well. Set pan of popcorn in hot water to prevent it from hardening while forming shapes. Lightly butter hands. Shape popcorn into eight 4-1/2 inch flat circles for pilgrim faces, using 1 cup popcorn mixture for each face. Make features for faces from black shoestring licorice, jelly beans, gumdrops or other small candies, using some of the hot syrup for "glue".

Priscilla's Hat — Cut two rectangles, one from white construction paper and one from black construction paper, each 8-1/2 x 5-1/2 inches. Fold long edge of each rectangle back one inch. Put black paper on top of white paper. Attach edge of hat that is folded back to face with roundheaded pins. Bend two lower back corners of rectangle forward. Make a bow out of white ribbon.

*licorice strings, gumdrops, jelly beans, black, white and yellow construction paper, cardboard, black crepe paper, ribbon and roundheaded pins.

John's Hat — Cut a 6-1/2 x 2-1/2 inch rectangle out of cardboard. Round off ends of one 6-1/2 inch side to form front of brim. On opposite 6-1/2 inch side, 1-1/4 inches from each edge, cut 1 inch up toward curved brim side. Then cut straight across so there is a 4 x 1 inch rectangle cut out of the straight side. Cover both sides of brim with black crepe paper. Outline crown of hat on another piece of cardboard, using a 4 inch base, tapered up about 4 inches toward a top of about 2-1/4 inches. Cover with crepe paper. Cut 1/2 inch square yellow buckle. Glue to crown. Fit two sections of hat together atop pilgrim face. Attach with pins.

Popcorn Cornucopias — Popcorn mixture may also be shaped into 8 cornucopias. Lightly butter the insides of 8 10-ounce cone-shaped paper cups. Press 1 cup popcorn mixture into each cup. Leave center hollow. After shaping cornucopia cones, allow them to set until cool and hard. Gently peel paper away. Fill cornucopias with assorted candies and nuts.

FALL FANTASY

One trip to a craft shop for materials and you're ready to create a fall arrangement of popcorn mums and cattails. See illustration on page 82.

5 qts. popped, unsalted popcorn (about 3/4 cup kernels)
white craft glue
styrofoam balls, four 2-1/2 in. and one 3 in. diameters
stems and calyxes from 12 plastic flowers (about 8 in. long)
1 can (6 ozs.) canary yellow matte-finish craft spray paint
4 artificial cattail stems with flat leaves (about 12 in. long)
1 can (6 ozs.) harvest brown matte-finish craft spray paint
styrofoam piece, 3/4 in. thick, to fit inside container
compote-type container (about 3 in. high)
1 bunch brown, dried, bearded wheat
wooden craft picks, 3 in. and 6 in. lengths
spool wire
wire cutters
Olive green velour ribbon, 1-1/2 in. wide, 26 in. long

Popcorn Mums — Form at least 7 blossoms by gluing popped popcorn kernels to one another. Make 1 mum 1-1/2 inches in diameter, 2 mums 2 inches, and 4 mums 3 inches. For 5 other blossoms, glue popcorn to the styrofoam balls. Set blossoms aside and let dry overnight. Insert a plastic stem with calyx into each mum. Spray mums thoroughly with yellow paint and let dry.

Popcorn Cattails — Thread between 8 and 15 popped popcorn kernels, one at a time, on each artificial stem above leaves. Spray cattails brown and set aside to dry.

Arrangement — Cut styrofoam to fit inside container bowl and glue in place. Separate some of the wheat into small bunches of spikes. Secure to short picks with wire. Begin arranging by inserting cattails in styrofoam at the center. Make them the highest point of the arrangement. Insert 3 smallest mums next, toward the top at varying heights. Put in 4 medium-size mums around the center and 5 large mums at the bottom. (Cut stems, or wire picks to stems as needed to get desired heights.) Fill in with wheat around entire piece.

Make a bow of ribbon, gathering it in the center with wire. Secure to a short pick. Stick into styrofoam at bottom of piece in focal center of arrangement.

QUICK TRICKS FOR CHRISTMAS DECORATIONS

Don't fail to check the directions in Popcorn Confections, page 35, for instructions on glazing and molding popcorn.

Use both white and tinted popcorn balls in a wicker cornucopia.

Form popcorn balls around candy canes. Hang them on the Christmas tree.

Trim an old fashioned Christmas tree with garlands of popcorn and cranberries. String them using a needle and strong thread.

Wrap balls of popcorn in colored transparent wrap and fasten on a circle of cardboard or wire to fashion a wreath. Add a bow.

Form a large popcorn ball and a smaller one. Press together to form a snowman. Dip candied fruit or gum drops in corn syrup and stick on for facial features. Place the large ball in a brandy snifter so it will stand up. Add hats and scarves.

Press silver dragees into popcorn balls before wrapping them in plastic wrap. Tie with red and green ribbons. Decorate the bows with dainty sprigs of mistletoe or holly. Suspend them appropriately overhead or hang on your tree.

POPCORN JINGLE BELLS

3 qts. popped popcorn
1 pkg. (10-1/2 ozs.) or 6 cups miniature marshmallows
1/2 cup red cinnamon candies
1/4 cup butter
1/2 tsp. salt
red food coloring
3 bars (1-3/8 ozs. ea.) milk chocolate
pipe cleaners
ribbon

Keep popcorn hot in 200°F oven. Measure marshmallows, cinnamon candies, butter and salt into heavy saucepan. Cook over low heat, stirring occasionally, until marshmallows are melted. Tint pink with food coloring. Pour mixture over popcorn. Stir gently to coat. Shape mixture into bells. A coffee cup may be used to form the bell and a saucer to form bell's lip as follows. Lightly butter inside of cup to keep corn from sticking. (Also lightly butter hands for working with hot popcorn.) Press mixture into cup to form bell and

onto saucer to form bell's lip. Quickly place 1/2 milk chocolate bar between bell and lip. Press together.

When bell has set, use a metal skewer to make hole through center of lip and bell in order to insert pipe cleaner for clapper. Ribbon may be attached to pipe cleaner ends on top of bells and arranged in different lengths for hanging if this is desired. Makes 6 to 8 bells.

SHOOTING STARS

For the small fry, this is a big hit. You will find it described again along with other party ideas in the Kids' Cookbook by Nitty Gritty.

Spread out a clean sheet on the floor. Put an electric popcorn popper in the middle and plug it in. Have the children sit in a circle (not too close) around the popper. Put the popcorn in the popper but leave off the lid. The young ones will love to watch the popcorn fireworks. After the shower of fireworks (popcorn) put the popcorn in a big brown bag. Add butter and salt. shake and serve. Remember to unplug the popper!

POPCORN FOR THE BIRDS

Give the birds a treat during the bleak winter months and you can have the added pleasure of watching them enjoy it. Thread a needle with nylon cord or dental floss and string alternately with popped corn and bacon or suet cut into small pieces. Hang the feast from your deck or porch, or a tree where you can see the activity from your window.

GROWING YOUR OWN POPCORN

Plant popcorn seeds about 12 inches apart in a sunny spot. For good pollination, plant at least three rows, leaving 18 to 24 inches between each row. (A word of caution—avoid planting popcorn and regular corn close together as it causes the regular corn to be tough.)

Popcorn takes at least 3 months to grow. The ears are ready for picking when the stalks are brown and dried out. Leave the husks on the ears and store them in a cool, dry place for about 1 month. Then remove the kernels and store them in a tightly sealed container until popping time.

If you can't find popcorn seeds in your area they can be ordered from the W. Atlee Burpee Company, Phildephia, Pennsylvania, 19132; or Clinton, Iowa, 52732; or Riverside, California, 92502.

Index

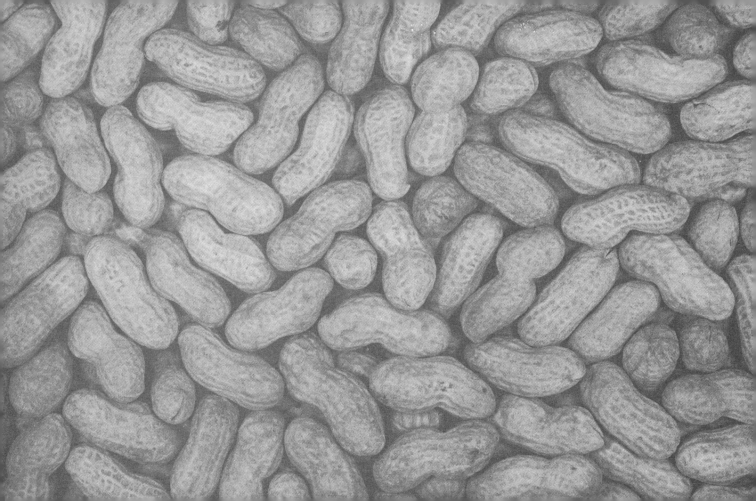

books designed with giving in mind

Kid's Pets Book
Make It Ahead
    French Cooking
Soups & Stews
Crepes & Omelets
Microwave Cooking
Vegetable Cookbook
Kid's Arts and Crafts
Bread Baking
The Crockery Pot Cookbook
Kid's Garden Book
Classic Greek Cooking

The Compleat American
    Housewife 1776
Low Carbohydrate Cookbook
Kid's Cookbook
Italian
Cheese Guide & Cookbook
Miller's German
Quiche & Souffle
To My Daughter, With Love
Natural Foods
Chinese Vegetarian
Jewish Gourmet
Working Couples

Mexican
Sunday Breakfast
Fisherman's Wharf Cookbook
Charcoal Cookbook
Ice Cream Cookbook
Hippo Hamburger
Blender Cookbook
The Wok, a Chinese Cookbook
Cast Iron Cookbook
Japanese Country
Fondue Cookbook
Food Processor Cookbook
Peanuts & Popcorn

from nitty gritty productions

GOOBER PEAS   Confederate soldiers' nonsense song, by A. E. Blackmar

Sitting by the roadside on a summer day,
Chatting with my mess-mates, passing time away.
Lying in the shadow underneath the trees,
Goodness, how delicious, eating goober peas!

Chorus: Peas! Peas! Peas! Peas! eating goober peas!
Goodness, how delicious, eating goober peas!

When a horseman passes, the soldiers have a rule
To cry out at their loudest "Mister, here's your mule;"
But another pleasure enchantinger than these
Is wearing out your grinders eating goober peas!

Just before the battle the Gen'ral hears a row,
He says, "The Yanks are coming, I hear their rifles now."
He turns around in wonder, and what d'you think he sees?
The Georgia militia, eating goober peas!

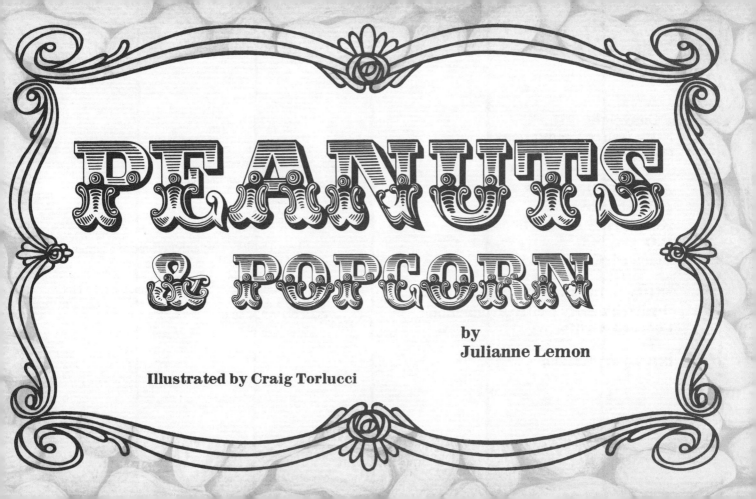

PEANUTS & POPCORN

by
Julianne Lemon

Illustrated by Craig Torlucci

A Nitty Gritty Book*
Published by
Nitty Gritty Productions
P.O. Box 5457
Concord, California 94524

*Nitty Gritty Books — Trademark
Owned by Nitty Gritty Productions
Concord, California

ISBN 0-911954-40-6

Library of Congress Cataloging in Publication Data

Lemon, Julianne.
    Peanuts and popcorn.

    Issued with the author's Popcorn and peanuts;
inverted text.
    Includes index.
    1. Cookery (Peanuts)   2. Popcorn.   I. Title
TX803.P35L46   641.6'5'6596   77-2409
ISBN 0-911954-40-6

Table of Contents

Most of these recipes were developed and contributed by the National Peanut Council in Chicago, Illinois. We thank them for their help.

&ᕤ All About Peanuts ᕤ&

The peanut is not actually a "nut" but a legume, a member of the pea family. Its low, bush-like plant bears small yellow flowers that become pods. The branches carrying the pods elongate, bend down and push their pods into the ground. When the plant dies the mature peanuts (or ground nuts, as they are often called) are dug up.

Peanuts are an all-American nut, and one of the world's oldest foods. They were in the Americas long before Columbus set foot in the New World, probably growing first in Peru. Peanut shaped pottery and peanut designs have been found in ancient Peruvian tombs.

Spanish explorers came looking for gold not goobers, but they took the seeds home to Spain for planting. Spanish and Portuguese traders peddled them to nearby Africa in exchange for spices and elephant tusks. The Africans made peanuts a staple in their diet and a favorite food. They even worshiped the peanut along with certain other species of plant life they believed had souls. The Africans call peanuts goobers, originally nguba. It is one of the few African words still retained in the English language. Peanuts are also called ground peas and monkey nuts.

3

When the 18th and 19th century slave traders came to America with black slaves they brought along the cheapest food available — peanuts. Some of the seeds made it ashore and were planted near the slave quarters on the large Southern plantations. They were considered a food only for the poor. It took the Civil War, the circus and baseball to spread the popularity of peanuts in the United States. Union soldiers sampled the nourishing nuts during the War, and in some instances returned home with a taste for the Confederate's "goober peas."

After the Civil War when the boll weevil wiped out the cotton crops, Southern farmers had to find another way to increase their income. The noted black scientist Dr. George Washington Carver suggested they plant peanuts. He pointed out that it would not only ease their financial pinch but that it would also revitalize the denurtured soil. This ecological pioneer, born a slave, is credited with finding over 300 uses for the peanut, shell and plant foliage.

❧ The Powerful Peanut ❧

Now, in an age when consumers are more aware and concerned about nutrition, peanuts are a wonder food. Besides rating high in protein they carry many of the essential B vitamins as well as vitamin E in the oil. As with some other foods such as wheat, and other legumes, such as beans, some of the essential amino acids which make up protein are found in varying amounts. That is why one plant protein combined with another (peanut butter and bread) multiplies the effectiveness of the protein. The peanut butter sandwich is an excellent combination of the plant proteins of the bread and the peanut. Add a glass of milk and an orange and you have a nutritionally balanced meal.

It is hardly news that the world is in the midst of a population explosion. As pasture land decreases, meat becomes less available and higher in price. In the years ahead we must find the means of supplying more and more people with nutritionally acceptable foods. Consider what the lowly peanut can do as a part of the solution. As the prices of other protein foods rise, peanuts are an exceptional way of introducing more protein into the diet. Nuts of all types, whether grown on trees or vegetatively, can replace meat or be used as meat extenders. They are an economical, easy-to-use, delicious body-building food.

And the versatile peanut has yet another bonus: peanuts yield a crop the same season they are planted. When you realize that land used for growing plant food will support 10 times as many people as land used for animal food, you will surely agree, we hit the jackpot with peanuts.

Raw, blanched, roasted, chopped, ground or crushed, peanuts are infiltrating stomachs of the world in ways George Washinton Carver never dreamed. For pure enjoyment, good nutrition or economic reasons, they deserve to be used even more. If you have never experimented cooking with peanuts beyond cookies or fudge — try some of the recipes in this book.

4

Know Your Peanuts

<u>In the Shell</u> — These peanuts are as taken from the soil except they have been cleaned and cured. They are available raw, roasted, or salted and roasted. Most roasted-in-shell peanuts are Virginia or Valencia types and are the kind associated with baseball and circuses.

<u>Raw Shelled</u> — The shell has been removed from the raw peanuts. They may be eaten raw or roasted, blanched or red-skinned. The largest use of these peanuts is in candy, cakes and breads.

<u>Blanched</u> — Peanuts have had their skin removed in this process. They can be unsalted or salted; raw or roasted.

<u>Cocktail</u> — Blanched or red-skin peanuts are cooked in hot vegetable oil and salted immediately upon removal from the hot oil. These peanuts have a variety of uses ranging from snacks to a main ingredient in recipes.

<u>Dry Roasted</u> — Peanuts are shelled, skinned and then roasted by dry heat. The salty flavor is obtained by an adhesive solution applied to the peanuts. They are ideal served as a snack.

5

Storage & Preparation of Raw Peanuts

Storing — In-shell peanuts keep better than shelled. Store them in a moisture proof container in a cool dark place or in the refrigerator, never at room temperature. Peanuts will become rancid in warm temperatures. Raw peanuts can kept in a fresh state indefinitely if placed in a freezer. They can be thawed and refrozen without loss of quality.

Blanching — In addition to the tough outer shell, peanuts have a thin inner lining or skin you may want to discard. Try one of these methods.

Boiling Water Method — Pour boiling water over the shelled nuts. For large quantities you may have to let them stand for about 1 minute at the most . . . the briefer the length of time the better. Drain and pour cold water over them to arrest further heating. Then pinch or rub off skins.

Oven Method — If you prefer, roast the peanuts at 350°F for 10 to 20 minutes and then rub off the skins.

6

<u>Roasting</u> — Peanuts lose nutrients when roasted but gain crispness and delicious flavor. While some believe there is little to be gained by home roasting, health addicts complain many commercially available roasted peanuts are actually deep fried at high temperatures in low-quality oil and oversalted as well. If you would like to roast peanuts in your own kitchen where you can control the temperature, quality of oil and amount of salt, here are two methods.

<u>Frying Pan Method</u> — Place shelled peanuts in a heavy frying pan over medium heat. Stir until a roasted aroma arises. Sprinkle on a few tea-spoons of pressed oil, coating all nuts. Stir in salt if desired.

<u>Oven Method</u> — To roast peanuts in the shell, keep your oven at 300°F and roast 30 to 40 minutes. Turn frequently to avoid scorching.

❧ Peanut Butter ❧

What was invented in 1890 by a St. Louis doctor, is found in 4 out of 5 American homes, is consumed at the rate of 235,000 TONS a year, is wonderfully nutritious and sticks to the roof of your mouth if it's good? You're right! Its's peanut butter, the most popular "nut" butter in the world.

Commercial peanut butters by Federal regulation must be at least 90% peanuts. The rest is hydrogenized fats (to prevent oil separation), sugar (for added sweetness and to mask the taste of inferior peanuts), emulsufiers (to protect us from oil separation), texturizers (to counteract the butter's natural tendency to stick to the roof of the mouth), and degermed peanuts (for long shelf life). Smooth and delicious as the commercial product may be, it is often made without the germ of the nut. This valuable portion contains minerals, vitamins, proteins and is literally fed to the birds.

It is possible to buy peanut butter made from 100% peanuts without additives. If you cannot find it on the grocery shelf, look in the refrigerated section.

For a consistantly high quality product, make your own freshly ground pure peanut butter. You can use a blender, a food processor or a home peanut

butter maker. Refrigerate the peanut butter during warm weather and give it a stir before using to redistribute the oils that rise to the top. Small trouble for a rich reward.

HOMEMADE PEANUT BUTTER

Measure into the container of a blender or food processor, 1 cup of freshly roasted or salted peanuts and 1-1/2 tablespoons peanut oil. Blend the mixture until it is smooth. Gradually add, with the blender turned on, another 1-1/2 tablespoons oil or enough to make the peanut butter the proper consistency. Add 1/2 teaspoon salt if the peanuts are unsalted. (If you wish to omit the oil you may. It simply makes a creamier more spreadable butter.)

9

➷ Cocktail Goodies ➹

There is nothing provincial about the peanut. They are munched in cocktail lounges from Hong Kong to Istanbul, from Buenos Aires to Paris. In France's best restaurants, a dish of peanuts, along with a few salted olives, often appear with the menus. In Mexico, spicy peanuts known as cachuetes (see page 12) can call for a lot of margaritas. Even a bowl of plain salted peanuts adds something special to cocktail time. That it adds significant nutrition also, as the chart below shows, is just an added attraction.

Nutritive Value of an Average Serving (3/4 oz.) of Salted Peanuts

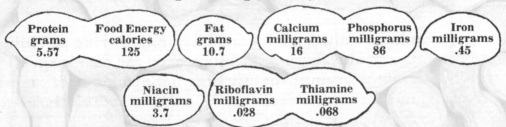

Protein grams 5.57 · Food Energy calories 125 · Fat grams 10.7 · Calcium milligrams 16 · Phosphorus milligrams 86 · Iron milligrams .45 · Niacin milligrams 3.7 · Riboflavin milligrams .028 · Thiamine milligrams .068

If you are ready to expand your "a little something before" repertoire, here are some unique additions.

CACAHUETES

Keep the Margaritas coming when you serve these spicy baked peanuts. They hail from Oaxaca, Mexico.

20 small 1-in. long dried red chile peppers
4 cloves crushed garlic
2 tbs. olive oil
2 lbs. blanched, salted peanuts
1 tsp. course salt
1 tsp. chili powder

In a heavy pan heat chilies, garlic and olive oil, stirring so chilies won't scorch. Add peanuts and stir. Spread the mixture on the cookie sheet. Bake in a 350°F oven five minutes or until slightly brown. Sprinkle with salt and chili powder. Mix well and store in a covered jar for a day or more before serving.

12

CHUTNEY PEANUT DIP

Serve with celery and carrot sticks, apple or pear wedges or cubes of banana.

1/2 cup peanut butter
1/2 cup sour cream
2 tbs. milk
1/2 cup chopped chutney
1 tsp. Worcestershire sauce
3 to 4 drops hot pepper sauce
1/4 tsp. seasoned salt

13

Blend together peanut butter, sour cream and milk until smooth. Stir in chutney, Worcestershire sauce, hot pepper sauce and salt. Makes 1-1/2 cups.

 Did you know that March is NATIONAL PEANUT MONTH and has been observed every year since 1941? No need to send cards — just think goobers!

NUTTY SPICE BALL

Serve with an assortment of fresh fruits, crackers, whatever your little heart desires.

2 pkgs. (8 ozs. ea.) cream cheese, softened
1 pkg. (4 oz.) blue cheese, crumbled
1 tbs. shredded orange peel
1 cup chopped peanuts
3/4 tsp. cinnamon
1/8 tsp. nutmeg
1/8 tsp. cloves

14

Whip cream cheese and blue cheese until light and fluffy. Stir in orange peel. Shape into a ball and chill. Toss together peanuts, cinnamon, nutmeg and cloves. Just before serving roll cheese ball in peanut mixture.

A DATE WITH PEANUTS

Guess how many individual canapes this makes?

20 pitted dates
20 whole salted peanuts
20 uncooked bacon strips (approximately 2-1/2 in. long)
20 toothpicks

15

Stuff dates with peanuts. Wrap with bacon strips, and secure with toothpicks. Bake 20 minutes in a 350°F oven. Cool before serving.

HINDU EGGS

A truly exotic looking and tasting appetizer that can be assembled well ahead of the frying time.

8 hard-cooked eggs
1 cup (4 ozs.) shredded
　　Swiss cheese
1/3 cup mayonnaise
2 tbs. chopped green onion

3/4 tsp. curry powder
1 tsp. salt
1 can (6-1/2 ozs.) peanuts, finely chopped
peanut oil
chopped chutney

16

Peel eggs and put through sieve. Stir in cheese, mayonnaise, onion, curry and salt. Using about 2 tablespoons for each, form mixture into egg shapes. Roll and press in chopped peanuts. Cover and chill about 1 hour. Heat peanut oil to 400°. Deep fry eggs until golden, about 2 to 3 minutes. Drain on absorbent toweling. Serve hot with chutney. Makes about 1-1/2 dozen.

PEANUTTY SALMON BALL

This pretty appetizer always makes a hit, especially with men.

1 can (16 ozs.) salmon
1 pkg. (8 ozs.) cream cheese
1 tbs. lemon juice
2 tsp. grated onion
1 tsp. prepared horseradish
1/4 tsp. salt
1/4 tsp. liquid smoke
1 cup finely chopped peanuts
1 tbs. minced fresh parsley

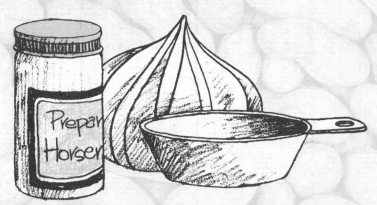

Drain and flake salmon removing skin and bones. Combine cream cheese lemon, onion, horseradish, salt and liquid smoke. Mix thoroughly. Chill several hours. When ready to serve add peanuts. If mixture is quite stiff peanuts may have to be worked in as mixture is shaped into a ball. Roll in parsley and serve with crackers.

TIGER

Breads & Muffins

Think about using peanuts and peanut butter frequently in your baking. Remember, combining protein-packed peanuts with other grains forms a protein partnership that satisfies nutritional needs at bargain prices. Important as this is, once you smell the aroma of Marvelous Muffins or Peanut Butter Banana Bread baking you will probably be contemplating eating enjoyment even more than good health.

Peanut meal can be used to boost the nutritional level of baked goods and lend delicious taste also. It is made of finely ground peanuts and is sometimes sold as peanut flour. It is rich in protein, vitamin B1, riboflavin and niacin like the peanut. Try using 1/4 cup peanut meal to 3/4 cup wheat flour in bread and cookie recipes. This meal is available roasted or unroasted. The roasted has a more distinctive nutty flavor.

MARVELOUS MUFFINS

High fiber content plus delicious flavor. Bake a double batch and warm them up for several mornings' breakfast.

1-1/4 cups flour
1 cup whole bran cereal
3 tbs. sugar
3 tsp. baking powder
1/3 cup chopped salted peanuts

1 egg
1 cup (2 very ripe) bananas, mashed
1/4 cup milk
1/4 cup butter or margarine, melted

20

In a medium bowl stir together flour, bran, sugar, baking powder and peanuts. In a smaller bowl beat egg slightly. Beat in bananas, milk and butter. Add all at once to flour mixture. Stir just until dry ingredients are moistened—ignore the lumps. Turn into buttered, medium-size muffin pan cups, filling them 1/2 full. Bake in a 400°F oven about 20 minutes. Serve at once or reheat to serve several mornings. Makes 12 muffins.

PEANUT BUTTER APPLE MUFFINS

Muffins lift everyday meals out of the ordinary by adding a "something special" touch. That's a nice return for so little effort.

2 cups sifted all-purpose flour
4 tsp. baking powder
3/4 tsp. salt
3/4 tsp. cinnamon
1/4 tsp. nutmeg
1/4 cup shortening

1/4 cup peanut butter
6 tbs. sugar
1 egg
1 cup milk
3/4 cup chopped raw apple

Sift together flour, baking powder, salt, 1/2 teaspoon cinnamon and nutmeg. Cream shortening and peanut butter together thoroughly. Gradually add 4 tablespoons sugar. Beat until fluffy. Add egg and beat well. Stir in milk and apple. Add flour mixture all at once. Stir just enough to moisten dry ingredients. Fill greased muffin tins two-thirds full. Blend together remaining 2 tablespoons sugar and remaining 1/4 teaspoon cinnamon. Sprinkle on tops of muffin batter. Bake in 400°F oven 20 to 25 minutes. Makes 15 to 18 muffins.

APRICOT PEANUT BREAD

For a lunch bag treat spread two slices with cream cheese in the middle.

1-1/4 cups apricot nectar
1-1/4 cups sugar
1 cup snipped dried apricots
1/2 cup <u>each</u> golden raisins and shredded coconut
1 tsp. almond flavoring
2 cups sifted flour
3 tsp. baking powder
1/2 tsp. salt
1/2 cup milk
1 egg, slightly beaten
2 tbs. peanut oil
1 cup chopped salted peanuts

22

In a medium size saucepan combine 1 cup apricot nectar, 1/4 cup sugar, apricots, raisins, coconut and almond flavoring. Bring to a boil. Remove from

heat and allow to cool. Sift together flour, remaining 1 cup sugar, baking powder and salt. Combine milk, egg and oil. Add egg mixture and remaining 1/4 cup apricot nectar to dry ingredients. Beat till smooth. Fold in apricot-raisin mixture and peanuts. Turn into greased and floured 9 x 5 x 3 inch loaf pan. Bake in 350°F oven 1 hour or until loaf tests done. Cool in pan for 10 minutes. Remove to cake rack to finish cooling. Makes 1 loaf.

PEANUT BUTTER BANANA BREAD

This is a wonderful bread toasted and topped with butter, but it can only be improved by putting more peanut butter on top.

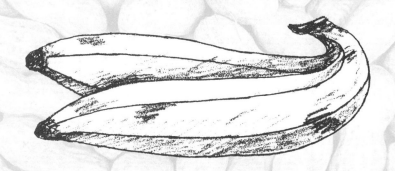

2 pkgs. dry yeast
1/3 cup warm water
3/4 cup peanut butter
1/2 cup brown sugar
2 large mashed bananas
1 egg
1 cup scalded milk, cooled
1-1/2 tsp. salt
6 to 7 cups all-purpose flour

24

Dissolve yeast in warm water and let sit until it is bubbly. Blend peanut butter and sugar together in large bowl. Beat until creamy. Stir in mashed bananas, egg, cooled milk, dissolved yeast and salt. Blend well. Add 2 cups of flour and beat well. Stir in enough additional flour to make a stiff dough. Turn

out onto a lightly floured board. Knead about 10 minutes, adding more flour as needed to keep dough from sticking. When dough is smooth and elastic, place in a large greased bowl. Turn to grease the top of dough. Cover and let rise in a warm place until doubled in bulk, about 1-1/2 hours. Punch down and divide dough in half. Shape each half and place in a greased loaf pan. Cover and let rise until doubled again. Bake in preheated 350°F oven 40 to 45 minutes. Remove from pans and cool on rack. Makes 2 loaves.

Note — You might like to do some experimenting here by increasing the nutritional value of the flour. Try substituting one cup of peanut meal, soy or whole wheat flour for all-purpose flour.

{ Did you know THE PEANUT GALLERY is the name applied to the top gallery in the theater where the cheaper seats are located? The name came from the practice of those sitting there eating peanuts and throwing shells on the stage. }

PEANUT BUTTER COFFEE CAKE

Great to make when you have to host the committee meeting.

1-1/2 cups packed brown sugar
1/2 cup all-purpose flour
3/4 cup peanut butter
2 tbs. butter, melted
1/4 cup shortening
2 eggs

2 cups flour
2 tsp. baking powder
1/2 tsp. baking soda
1/2 tsp. salt
1 cup milk

Mix 1/2 cup brown sugar, flour, 1/4 cup peanut butter and butter together until crumbly. Set aside. Cream remaining 1/2 cup peanut butter and shortening together. Beat in remaining 1 cup brown sugar. Add eggs, one at a time, beating until fluffy. Stir together flour, baking powder, soda and salt. Add alternately with milk to creamed mixture. Beat after each addition. Spread in greased 13 x 9 x 2 inch baking pan. Top with crumbly mixture. Bake at 375°F 30 to 35 minutes. Makes about 16 servings.

PEANUT BUTTER PANCAKES

If waffles are your choice, add one more egg and 2 tablespoons oil to the batter and bake in a waffle iron.

1 cup all-purpose flour
2 tbs. sugar
2 tsp. baking powder
1/2 tsp. salt
1 beaten egg
1 cup milk
1/3 cup chunky peanut butter
1 tbs. peanut oil

Thoroughly stir together in mixing bowl the flour, sugar, baking powder and salt. Beat egg with peanut butter until blended. Add milk and oil. Add all at once to dry ingredients. Bake on hot, lightly greased griddle or skillet. Makes six to eight 4-inch pancakes.

❦ Soups & Salads ❦

Versatility is the name of the game when cooking with peanuts. Perhaps you've never thought of using them for salads or soups but the possibilities are endless. It can be something as simple as tossing a handful of peanuts into your salad, or sprinkling some crushed nuts on soup as a garnish. You will be adding interest, texture and distinctive flavor. In Southeast Asia peanuts star in innocent looking but fiery salads. In South America as well as New Orleans peanut soups are favorites. The soup and salad examples that follow are designed for American food tastes but offer some wide-ranging possibilities

If you haven't tried peanut oil you should. The peanut yields this light bland oil that is good for salads and cooking and particularly good for frying. Buy it freshly pressed, filtered rather than refined and without preservatives and solvents.

POT-OF-GOLD PEANUT SOUP

Serve this as a great beginning or a satisfying entree.

4 pkgs. (1/4 oz. ea.) dried mushrooms
8 cups water
3 tbs. instant chicken bouillon
1 dried red chili pepper or
    1/4 tsp. dried crushed red pepper
1/3 cup pearl barley

1 cup chunky peanut butter
1 pkg. (10 ozs.) frozen chopped
    broccoli, thawed and drained
2 tbs. fresh lemon juice
2 tbs. chopped parsley

Cover dried mushrooms with a small amount of water. Soak about five minutes or until rehydrated. Drain. Mix 8 cups water, bouillon and pepper together in a large saucepan over medium heat. Bring to a boil and stir in barley. Cover and simmer 1 hour or until barley is tender. Remove from heat. Blend peanut butter into mixture with a wire whip until smooth. Return to heat and cook, stirring, until soup is thickened. Stir in broccoli and mushrooms. Simmer 3 to 5 minutes. Remove from heat. Add lemon juice and parsley. Serve hot. Makes about 8 cups.

CREAMY PEANUT SOUP

A rich, thoroughly elegant soup.

2 carrots, chopped
2 stalks celery, chopped
2 cups water
1 jar (12 ozs.) creamy peanut butter
1 pt. heavy cream
1-1/2 cups milk
1-1/2 tsp. salt
1/8 tsp. cayenne pepper
crushed peanuts for garnish

Boil vegetables in water until tender. Puree with a little liquid in a blender. Pour pureed mixture into large pan. Slowly add peanut butter. Stir over low heat until smooth. Blend in heavy cream. Add milk, salt and pepper. Continue stirring over medium heat until soup is hot but do not boil. Sprinkle crushed peanuts over top just before serving. Makes 6 servings.

KITCHEN SHELF SOUP

1/4 cup finely chopped onion
1 tbs. butter
1/2 cup creamy peanut butter
1 can (10-1/2 ozs.) cream of
    chicken soup

1 can (10-1/2 ozs.) cream of celery soup
2-1/4 cups milk
1/4 cup chopped salted peanuts

32   Saute onion in butter until tender. Stir in peanut butter. Cook several minutes. Blend in soups and milk. Add peanuts. Heat but do not boil. Garnish with paprika, parsley or more peanuts, if desired. Makes 6 to 8 servings.

PEANUT TOMATO SOUP

2 cans (10-1/2 ozs. ea.) tomato soup
1/4 cup peanut butter

1/4 tsp. basil
2 soup cans milk

Blend soup, peanut butter and basil in saucepan. Add milk gradually, stirring until evenly blended. Heat to serving temperature. Makes 4 servings.

PEANUT SUPER SALAD

This salad is hearty enough to be supper for four. Add an interesting roll or bread, and dessert if you're feeling sufficiently scrawny.

1/2 cup peanut oil
3 tbs. fresh lemon juice
1 tbs. white vinegar
1 tsp. sugar
1 tsp. coriander seed, crushed
1 tsp. cumin seed, crushed
1 clove garlic, crushed
1/2 tsp. salt

dash of cayenne pepper
8 cups broken salad greens
2 cups (1/4 lb.) sliced mushrooms
2 cups julienne-cut cooked
    pork, chicken, ham or beef
1-1/2 cups cocktail peanuts
orange slices
black olives

In a small glass jar, shake together oil, lemon juice, vinegar, sugar, coriander, cumin, garlic, salt and pepper. Chill. Just before serving toss greens, mushrooms, meat and peanuts with dressing to coat. Serve in a lettuce cup garnished with orange slices or black olives or maybe both. Why not?

PEANUT-PASTA SALAD

This pretty main dish salad is packed with good nutrition. Add a cup of soup, bread sticks and fresh fruit and you've got a great lunch.

1 pkg. (5 ozs.) corkscrew macaroni
1 pkg. (10 ozs.) frozen peas and carrots
1 cup cocktail peanuts
1 cup cubed cheddar cheese
2 hard-cooked eggs, chopped
2 tbs. minced onion

1 cup mayonnaise
1 tbs. prepared mustard
3 tbs. sweet pickle relish
1/2 tsp. salt
dash of cayenne pepper

34

Cook macaroni according to package directions. Drain and chill in cold water. Drain well. Cook peas and carrots according to package directions. Drain and chill in cold water. Drain well. Combine macaroni and vegetables in mixing bowl. Toss with peanuts, cheese, chopped eggs and onion. In a small bowl combine mayonnaise, mustard, relish, salt and cayenne. Stir into macaroni mixture. Chill until serving time. Makes approximately 6 cups.

MAKE AHEAD SPINACH SALAD

3/4 lb. fresh spinach
1/2 medium cucumber, thinly sliced
1/2 cup thinly sliced radishes
1/4 cup thinly sliced green or Bermuda onion
2 hard-cooked eggs, sliced
3/4 cup thick blue cheese dressing
    (found in the produce section of most markets)
5 slices bacon, crisply fried and crumbled
1/2 cup salted Spanish peanuts (the ones with the red skins)

Wash spinach well. Drain and pat dry. Tear spinach into bite-sized pieces. Arrange in a shallow salad bowl. Over the spinach evenly layer cucumber slices, radishes, green onion and eggs. Spread dressing evenly over top, cover and chill as long as 24 hours. Just before serving sprinkle with bacon and peanuts. Lift out each serving with a spoon and fork, and be sure to get some of each layer of salad. Makes 6 servings.

PEANUT-DECKED BANANA SALAD

2 tbs. smooth peanut butter
1-1/2 tsp. grated orange peel
1-1/2 tsp. finely chopped
    crystalline ginger (optional)
2 medium bananas, split lengthwise
1/4 cup mayonnaise

1 tbs. orange juice
chopped peanuts
fresh fruits in season
Creamy Orange Dressing

Combine peanut butter, orange peel and ginger. Spread 1 tablespoon of mixture on two banana halves. Top each with remaining halves. Cut into 4 pieces each. Dip into combined mayonnaise and orange juice. Roll in chopped peanuts to coat. Serve on salad greens with other fresh fruit. Top with Creamy Orange Dressing. Makes 8 servings.

Creamy Orange Dressing — In a small bowl combine 1/2 cup evaporated milk, 1/2 cup smooth peanut butter, 1 tbs. grated orange peel and 1/4 cup orange juice. Chill.

PEAR AND CHICKEN NUT MOLD

Cheese nut balls make an unexpected and satisfying garnish for a fresh fruit salad too.

1 pkg. (8 ozs.) cream cheese, softened
1-1/2 cups chopped peanuts
1 can (1 lb. 13 ozs.) pear halves
2 pkgs. (3 ozs. ea.) lime flavored gelatin
1 cup minced chicken

38

Whip cream cheese until light and fluffy. Stir in 1 cup chopped peanuts. Shape into 16 balls. Roll balls in remaining 1/2 cup chopped peanuts and set aside. Drain pears reserving liquid. In a large bowl dissolve gelatin in 2 cups boiling water. Add enough water to pear liquid to measure 2 cups. Add to gelatin mixture. Place 8 cheese balls in bottom of an 8-cup mold. Pour about 1 cup gelatin into mold. Chill until almost set. Chill remaining gelatin to consistency of unbeaten egg white. Stir in chicken. Place one cheese ball into indentation of each of 8 pear halves. Stand stuffed pear halves around outside

edge of mold, cheese ball facing out. Chop any remaining pear halves and stir into gelatin-chicken mixture. Pour into mold. Chill until set. Unmold onto salad greens. Garnish with fresh vegetable relishes. Looks gorgeous and makes 8 servings.

DIXIE COLESLAW

Peanut halves add a wonderful texture contrast to this salad and make peanut lovers very happy.

2 cups finely chopped cabbage
1/4 cup chopped green pepper
1/2 cup chopped celery
1/2 cup salted peanut halves
2 tbs. sugar
1/4 cup peanut oil
1/2 tsp. paprika
2 tbs. instant minced onion
1/4 cup vinegar
1/2 tsp. salt

Toss together cabbage, pepper, celery and peanuts. Combine remaining ingredients. Pour over cabbage and toss well. Chill 1 hour before serving to 4 to 6 people.

40

PEANUT WALDORF SALAD

Another old favorite made even better with the addition of peanuts. When a variety of apples are in season, use several different ones in the same salad.

5 red apples
1 tbs. lemon juice
1 cup diced celery
1/2 cup chopped peanuts
2/3 cup mayonnaise
1/4 cup peanut butter

Core and dice unpeeled apples. Toss with lemon juice. Add celery and nuts. Blend a small amount of mayonnaise into peanut butter, then blend mixture into remaining mayonnaise. Combine dressing and salad ingredients. Serve on greens. Makes 6 servings.

 Egg salad takes on a new dimension when chopped peanuts are added.

❧ Vegetables ❧

What a difference a crunch makes! But the addition of peanuts to vegetable dishes means more than a mere texture treat. You are adding an exceptionally concentrated food rich in protein and fats, the polyunsaturated kind, and at bargin prices.

Another opportunity to add crunch is by perking up casseroles with a peanut topping. Try this combination: 1/4 cup chopped peanuts mixed with 1/4 cup cereal, bread crumbs or cracker crumbs and 2 tablespoons peanut oil. Sprinkle over the top of casserole just before it goes into the oven.

It's fun to experiment with sauces for vegetables. A delicious one can be quickly made by sauteeing chopped peanuts in butter until lightly browned. Stir in fresh lemon juice to taste and pour over hot vegetable. Be a little more elegant and blend sour cream in with the lemon juice to serve with broccoli, brussels sprouts or green beans.

The peanut has such verstility and combines well with so many other foods, it can be a happy discovery for the modern creative cook.

PEANUT VEGETABLE MEDLEY

No fresh vegetables in your refrigerator? Peanuts perk up frozen ones!

1 pkg. (10 ozs.) frozen chopped broccoli
1 pkg. (10 ozs.) frozen whole kernel corn
2 tbs. butter
2 tbs. minced onion
1/4 cup chopped green pepper
1 cup chopped tomato
1 cup chopped peanuts
1/2 tsp. salt
1/4 tsp. cayenne pepper

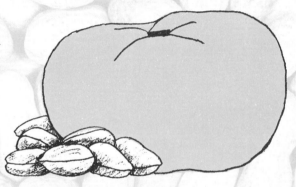

Cook broccoli and corn according to package directions. Drain and keep warm. In a small saucepan melt butter. Stir in onion and green pepper. Saute until tender. Stir onion and green pepper into cooked vegetables along with tomato, peanuts, salt and cayenne pepper. Makes 6 servings.

PEANUT BUTTER GLAZED CARROTS

A delicious glaze makes carrots something special.

1 lb. carrots (about 6) pared and sliced
2 tbs. butter
2 tbs. creamy peanut butter
1 tbs. flour
1/2 tsp. salt
1/4 tsp. ground ginger
1 cup orange juice

Cook carrots in boiling, salted water until tender. Drain well. Melt butter and peanut butter in saucepan. Remove from heat. Blend in flour, salt and ginger. Stir in orange juice gradually. Cook over medium heat, stirring constantly, until sauce thickens and boils 1 minute. Stir in drained carrots. Heat and serve. Makes 6 servings.

CAULIFLOWER-PEANUT POLONAISE

It's the crunch that does it!

1 medium head cauliflower
1/2 cup butter
1 tbs. fresh lemon juice
1 tbs. chopped parsley
1/3 cup toasted fresh bread crumbs
1 cup coarsely chopped peanuts

46

Wash and separate cauliflower into flowerettes. Cook in 1-inch boiling salted water over medium heat, 8 to 10 minutes or until tender. Drain well. Melt butter. Add lemon juice and parsley. Stir in bread crumbs and peanuts. Pour over cooked cauliflower and toss to coat. Makes 6 servings.

SPINACH CONTINENTAL

1 lb. fresh spinach
1/2 cup peanut oil
1/4 cup chopped onion
1 medium tomato, cut into wedges
2 or 3 tbs. soy sauce
1/8 tsp. cayenne pepper
3 tbs. peanut butter
3/4 cup peanuts

Wash spinach removing tough stems. Drain and pat dry. In large skillet saute onion and tomato in 1/4 cup oil. When tomato is tender, remove from skillet. Add remaining oil to skillet. Cook spinach in oil until tender. Push to one side. Stir in soy sauce and cayenne. Add peanut butter into liquid in pan. Heat stirring constantly until liquid thickens. Stir in peanuts. Return tomato and onion to skillet with spinach and toss until ingredients are mixed. You may want salt and pepper. Makes 4 servings.

FAVORITE STUFFED EGGPLANT

You can't ask more of a vegetable dish than this . . . delicious, impressive looking, economical and easy to prepare.

1 medium to large eggplant
3 tbs. peanut oil
1/4 cup butter
1/2 cup chopped onions
1 clove garlic, crushed
1 medium tomato, chopped
1/4 tsp. dried thyme
1/8 tsp. cayenne
1/2 tsp. salt
1 cup chopped peanuts
1-1/2 cups fresh bread crumbs
1 cup shredded mozzarella cheese

48

Cut eggplant in half lengthwise. Remove the center by cutting around the

edge with a grapefruit knife, leaving a 1/4-inch shell. Chop eggplant pulp and set aside. Heat oil in a skillet. Place eggplant shells cut side down in skillet. Cover and cook over moderate heat 5 minutes. Turn shells over, rolling them in oil to coat outside. Cover and cook 5 minutes. Drain shells on paper towels. Arrange in a shallow baking dish. Drain off remaining oil. Add butter, onion and garlic and cook until onion is tender. Add chopped eggplant, tomato and seasonings. Cook over moderate heat until eggplant is soft, approximately 5 minutes. Stir occasionally. Stir in peanuts and bread crumbs. Generously spoon mixture into eggplant shells. Bake in a preheated 400°F oven 15 minutes. Remove from oven and sprinkle with cheese. Return to oven until cheese is melted. Makes 4 servings.

49

{ Great love affairs have been based on a mutual passion for a mayonnaise, peanut butter and sliced banana sandwich. The longevity of the affairs has not been recorded, but the passion for the sandwich survives. }

HAM STUFFED SQUASH

Prepare early in the day and refrigerate until half an hour before serving time.

2 acorn squash
2 tbs. butter
2 cups (about 3/4 lb.) minced baked ham
2 tbs. minced onion
1 tbs. firmly packed brown sugar
1 tbs. grated orange peel

1/4 cup orange juice
1 tsp. salt
1 cup peanuts, chopped
1-1/2 tbs. melted butter
1/4 cup chopped parsley

50

Preheat oven to 350°F. Halve squash and remove seeds. Place squash, cut side down, on greased baking pan and bake about 45 minutes or until tender. Scoop pulp out of squash into a mixing bowl leaving a thin shell. Saute ham and onion in butter and stir into squash along with brown sugar, orange peel, juice, salt and peanuts. Refill shells with mixture and drizzle with melted butter. Bake 20 to 30 minutes in preheated oven or until heated through. Garnish with chopped parsley and whole peanuts. 4 servings.

STUFFED POTATOES GOOBER STYLE

For prettier stuffed potatoes always bake an extra potato so you'll have more stuffing to pile back into the shells.

7 potatoes
1/4 cup melted butter or margarine
light cream or milk

1/2 cup chopped salted peanuts
seasoned salt
paprika

51

Bake potatoes. Immediately cut a slice from the top of each. Scoop out potato leaving shells intact. Mash potatoes well. Add butter and enough cream to make potatoes light and fluffy. Fold in peanuts and season to taste. Pile fluffy potato mixture back into 6 shells. Brush with a little melted butter and dust lightly with paprika. Serve at once or heat until lightly browned in a 450°F oven. Makes 6 servings.

Note — Chopped peanuts are also delicious on buttered baked potatoes or sprinkled over baked potatoes topped with sour cream.

ꙮ Main Dishes ꙮ

While we may think of peanuts as snack food, in other parts of the world they are a crucial part of the diet. When you are feeling the squeeze of inflated food prices, remember the peanut. This ideal source of inexpensive protein combines with economical cuts of meat and poultry, other grains or dairy products in exciting main dishes. It is a protein partnership that means good taste and good health, economically.

It is worth remembering that while the body can store fat and certain amounts of sugar, it has no facilities for storing protein. We don't need large amounts, however. For the average adult, from five to seven ounces of protein per day is enough. Happily, peanuts can help you supply this need economically and with great versatility.

PEANUT MEAT LOAF

Always a family favorite, this version has a crunchy glazed outside.

1 lb. ground beef
1 lb. ground ham
2 cups crushed corn flakes
2 eggs, beaten
1/2 cup chopped onions
1/4 tsp. pepper
1/2 tsp. salt
2 cups chopped peanuts
2/3 cup brown sugar

54

Mix beef, ham, cornflakes, eggs, onions, pepper, salt and 1-1/2 cups peanuts together. Combine brown sugar and remaining 1/2 cup peanuts. Line the bottom and sides of a greased 9-inch loaf pan with the peanut-brown sugar mixture. Fill pan with the meat mixture. Bake in 375°F oven 1-1/4 hours. Carefully turn out onto serving platter, glazed-side up. Makes 8 to 10 servings.

PEANUT BROWN RICE ORIENTAL

Try this in your electric skillet. Good nutrition and so easy!

1-1/2 cups natural brown rice
1 can (11 ozs.) mandarin orange segments
1/2 cup soy sauce
3 cups water
1-1/2 tbs. butter
1 large clove garlic, crushed
1 cup thinly sliced celery

1/2 cup sliced green onions
1 cup salted peanuts
1 tbs. honey
1 tbs. lemon juice
1 can (1 lb.) bean sprouts, drained
3 tbs. chopped parsley

Measure rice into a large skillet. Drain oranges reserving 1/2 cup of the liquid. Set oranges aside. Add reserved liquid to rice. Stir in soy sauce, water, butter and garlic. Cover skillet. Simmer mixture about 45 minutes or until rice is tender and the liquid has been absorbed. Add celery, onion and peanuts during the last 5 minutes of cooking. Stir in honey, lemon juice, bean sprouts, reserved oranges and parsley. Serve immediately. Makes 6 servings.

CRISPY BAKED CHICKEN

An unusual and flavorful version of oven-fried chicken.

1 frying chicken, cut up
salt and pepper
3/4 cup flour
1 egg, beaten
1 cup orange marmalade
1 tsp. dry mustard
2 cloves garlic, crushed
1-1/2 cups peanuts, ground

56

Season chicken with salt and pepper. Put flour in a bag and add chicken parts, one at a time, shaking to coat. In a shallow dish combine egg, marmalade, mustard and garlic. Dip chicken in egg mixture to coat then roll in ground peanuts. Bake in 375°F oven 40 to 45 minutes or until fork tender. Makes about 4 servings.

HUNGARIAN HAM BUFFET

A faraway flavor for an economical stay-at-home dinner.

1 cup long grain brown rice
1 tbs. instant chicken bouillon
5 cups (about 1 lb.) shredded cabbage
1/3 cup chopped onion
1/4 cup butter
1 cup chopped ham

1 cup peanuts
1/2 cup seedless raisins
1 tsp. salt
1/4 tsp. cayenne pepper
1/2 cup light cream
1 egg, beaten

57

Cook rice according to package directions, adding bouillon to water. Drain well. In a large skillet, saute cabbage and onion in butter until tender. Stir in cooked rice, ham, peanuts, raisins, salt and cayenne. In a small bowl, combine cream and egg. Pour over cabbage mixture. Cook and stir until hot. Makes about 6 servings.

PEANUT FIESTA

A good casserole to stand on its own, or go along with oven-baked chicken.

1 can (4 ozs.) green chiles
2 cups milk
1 cup peanut butter
2 tsp. chili powder
1/2 tsp. salt

1/4 tsp. ginger
2 cloves garlic, crushed
1 cup (4 ozs.) shredded cheddar cheese
3 tbs. chopped parsley
3-1/2 cups cooked rice

58

Drain, seed and chop chiles. Gradually blend milk into peanut butter until smooth. Stir in chiles, chili powder, salt, ginger and garlic. Combine cheese and parsley. Spoon half of rice into a buttered 2-quart casserole. Pour half of peanut butter mixture over rice. Sprinkle with half of cheese and parsley. Repeat, omitting cheese and parsley. Heat in a 375°F oven 35 to 40 minutes or until hot. Sprinkle with remaining cheese and parsley. Let stand until cheese melts or return to oven to finish melting cheese. Garnish with extra parsley. Makes 6 to 8 servings.

PEANUT PROTEIN PATTIES

Panic not if your son says, "I'd like to bring a girl home for dinner, and she's a vegetarian." Try these. An interesting change from the ubiquitous hamburger.

5-1/2 cups soft whole wheat bread crumbs
2 cups cocktail peanuts, finely chopped
2 cups shredded American process cheese
1/2 cup onion, minced
2 tbs. chopped parsley
1 tsp. <u>each</u> paprika and ground coriander
1/2 cup milk
2 eggs, beaten
butter or peanut oil
Peanut Butter Sauce, page 61

60

In a bowl toss together 4 cups bread crumbs, peanuts, cheese, onion, parsley, paprika and coriander. Combine milk and eggs. Stir into bread mix-

ture. Divide mixture into 6 portions and shape into patties. Dip patties in remaining bread crumbs to coat. Heat butter or oil in a skillet over medium low heat. Cook patties until brown and thoroughly heated. Serve with Peanut Butter Sauce. Makes 6 servings.

Peanut Butter Sauce

1-1/4 cups milk
1/2 cup creamy peanut butter
2 tbs. soy sauce
1 clove garlic, crushed
dash of cayenne pepper

Combine ingredients in a small saucepan, over medium heat. Bring mixture to a boil and stir constantly until thickened. Serve over peanut burgers.

ORIENTAL CREPES

Don't pass by this elegant entree just because there are three parts to the recipe. Each step is simple and can be completed well ahead of serving time.

1/2 lb. cooked cut-up shrimp
1 cup peanuts, chopped
1/2 cup chopped celery
1/2 cup chopped water chestnuts
2 tbs. minced green onion
1-1/2 tbs. soy sauce

1 tbs. dry sherry
1/4 tsp. ground ginger
1/2 tsp. salt
Crepes, page 63
Mustard Sauce, page 63

62

Toss shrimp, peanuts, celery, water chestnuts, onion, soy sauce, sherry ginger and salt together in a bowl. Set aside while preparing crepes. When crepes are baked, spoon about 1/4 cup filling in the center of each crepe and roll up. Place seam side up in a large, lightly greased baking dish. Cover with foil. Bake in a 400°F oven about 20 minutes or until thoroughly heated. Serve with Mustard Sauce. Makes 12 crepes.

Crepes

1-1/2 cups flour	1/2 tsp. salt	2 eggs
1/2 tsp. baking powder	2 cups milk	2 tbs. butter

Combine ingredients in a bowl. Beat until smooth. Heat and lightly butter an 8 inch skillet. Pour 1/4 cup batter into skillet. Rotate so batter covers bottom. Cook crepe until lightly browned on both sides. Makes 12 crepes.

Mustard Sauce

2 cups sour cream	2 tbs. flour	1 cup milk
2 tsp. grated onion	2 tsp. dry mustard	2 egg yolks

In a saucepan, stir together sour cream, onion, flour and mustard. Blend in milk. Bring to a boil over medium heat, stirring constantly. Boil 1 minute. Lightly beat egg yolks with a little of the cooked mixture. Gradually stir back into saucepan. Serve warm sauce over filled crepes.

FRENCH OMELET WITH CURRIED PEANUT SAUCE

An easy to prepare sauce takes this omelet out of the ordinary. A perfect light dinner for the two of you, or for brunch or lunch, of course.

Curried Peanut Sauce, page 65
4 eggs
1 tbs. minced onion
1/4 tsp. salt
dash of white pepper
1 tbs. butter
6 slices bacon, cooked crisp and crumbled

Prepare sauce as directed. Keep warm while preparing omelet. Beat eggs just until blended, not foamy. Stir in onion, salt and pepper. Melt butter in an omelet pan or 8-inch skillet over low heat. Tilt pan to coat sides. Add egg mixture. Run spatula around edge, lifting egg to allow uncooked portion to flow underneath. Cook slowly until egg is set, but still shiny, and bottom is golden

brown. Sprinkle bacon on one half of omelet. Fold the other half over bacon. Turn onto heated platter. Serve with warm Curried Peanut Sauce.

Curried Peanut Sauce

1 cup (1/2 pt.) sour cream
1 tbs. flour
1 tsp. curry powder
1/4 tsp. powdered ginger
3/4 cup chopped peanuts

Combine sour cream, flour, curry and ginger. Bring to a boil over medium heat, stirring constantly. Boil 1 minute. Stir in peanuts. Place over hot water to keep warm while preparing omelet.

 Raw peanuts can be kept in a fresh state indefinitely if placed in a freezer.

ᎧᏍ Desserts ᎧᏍ

Since this is the absolute, hands-down sweetest peanut story we know, it seems fitting that it introduce the desserts:

A party crawling with celebrities and wits took place in New York in the twenties, and a shy, young Helen Hayes sat in a corner watching the scene. "Do you want a peanut?" asked a curly haired beautiful young man. He poured the peanuts from a crumpled paper bag into her trembling hand and added, "I wish they were emeralds." Naturally, she married him.

The line was repeated, committed to print and continued to haunt Charlie MacArthur. So depressed was the playwrite at being forever reminded of it that, at the end of World War II, returning from India and the Eastern Theater, he dumped a bag of emeralds in his wife's lap with the comment, "I wish they were peanuts."

CHOCOLATE POTS DE CREME

An elegant conclusion to a special dinner party.

1/2 cup milk
2 sqs. (1 oz. ea.) unsweetened chocolate
1 tsp. butter
3/4 cup confectioners' sugar
1/2 cup peanut butter

1 tsp. vanilla
2 egg yolks, beaten
2 egg whites
1/2 cup whipping cream, whipped
chopped peanuts

In a saucepan, over low heat, warm milk, chocolate and butter, stirring occasionally until chocolate is melted. Stir in sugar, peanut butter and vanilla until smooth. Spoon a little of the hot mixture into beaten egg yolks. Combine with the other ingredients in the saucepan. Continue to heat until just hot. Cover and cool. Beat egg whites until stiff and fold into peanut mixture. Fold in whipped cream. Divide mixture evenly into 6 individual pot de creme cups. Chill. Garnish each with a dollop of whipped cream and chopped peanuts. Makes 6 servings.

FLUFFY FROZEN PEANUT BUTTER PIE

A frozen-ahead dessert pie, so dear to the hearts of busy people.

1 9-inch graham cracker or regular crust
4 ozs. cream cheese, softened
1 cup confectioners' sugar
1/3 cup creamy peanut butter
1/2 cup milk
1 carton (9 ozs.) Cool Whip topping
1/4 cup finely chopped salted peanuts

69

Bake crust and cool. Whip cheese until soft and fluffy. Beat in sugar and peanut butter. Slowly add milk, blending thoroughly into mixture. Fold topping into mixture. Pour into baked pie shell. Sprinkle with chopped peanuts. Freeze until firm and serve. If not used the same day, wrap it well for the freezer.

TIN ROOF SUNDAE

No peanut book would be complete without this old-fashioned ice cream treat from the mid-west. Nothing to measure, cook or blend. Eyeball the proportions to suit your fancy.

For each serving fill a bowl with a fine quality vanilla ice cream. Spoon over a rich chocolate syrup. Scatter on, with abandon, salted Spanish peanuts.

70

Precautionary note — It should be considered close to illegal to substitute any other flavor for vanilla ice cream, hot fudge for the chocolate syrup or any peanut but the red-skinned Spanish kind.

ORANGE NUT CAKES

2 medium oranges
1 cup seedless raisins
3/4 cup finely chopped peanuts
2 cups flour
1 cup sugar
1 tsp. baking soda
1 tsp. salt

1/2 cup shortening
1/2 cup peanut butter
1 cup milk
2 eggs
1/3 cup sugar
1 tsp. cinnamon

Squeeze oranges, reserving juice. Remove membranes. Cut up peels and blend in a blender until finely chopped. Add raisins and continue blending until finely chopped. Stir in chopped peanuts. Set aside. In a mixing bowl stir together flour, sugar, baking soda and salt. Blend together shortening, peanut butter and 3/4 cup milk. Add to flour mixture and stir until blended. Beat in eggs and 1/4 cup milk. Stir in orange mixture. Spoon into 24 greased 2-1/4 x 1-1/4 inch cups. filling each 2/3 full. Bake in a 350°F oven 20 to 25 minutes. Remove cakes from pan and quickly dip into reserved orange juice to moisten outside. Roll in combined sugar and cinnamon. Makes 2 dozen cakes.

OLD FASHIONED PEANUT BARS

1/2 cup butter, softened
1 cup packed light brown sugar
1 egg
1 tsp. vanilla
1 tsp. rum extract
1 cup crushed graham crackers
1 cup flour

2 tsp. baking powder
1/2 tsp. salt
1 cup milk
1 cup chopped peanuts
1/2 cup seedless raisins
Peanut Velvet Frosting

72

In a mixing bowl, cream butter until light and fluffy. Beat in brown sugar, egg and extracts. Fold in crushed graham crackers. Sift together flour, baking powder and salt. Blend into creamed mixture alternately with milk. Stir in peanuts and raisins. Pour into greased 9 x 13 inch baking pan. Bake in 350°F oven 35 to 40 minutes. Frost with Peanut Velvet Frosting. Makes 24 bars.

Peanut Velvet Frosting — Heat 1/4 cup butter in saucepan over low heat until butter is light amber. Beat in 2 cups powdered sugar, 3 tablespoons milk, 1 teaspoon vanilla and a dash of salt. Add 1/2 cup peanut butter. Stir to blend.

BOYFRIEND COOKIES

1 cup butter
1-1/3 cups granulated sugar
1-1/3 cups firmly packed light brown sugar
2 eggs, unbeaten
1 tsp. vanilla
1-1/2 cups unsifted all-purpose flour
1 tsp. baking soda
3-1/2 cups rolled oats (quick or old fashioned)
1-1/2 cups chopped salted peanuts
1 pkg. (6 ozs.) chocolate bits

   Cream butter in a large mixing bowl. Slowly beat in sugars. Add unbeaten eggs and vanilla. Beat until fluffy. Sift flour with soda. Add oats. Stir into first mixture. Stir in chopped peanuts and chocolate bits. Drop rounded teaspoonfuls onto ungreased cookie sheet. Bake in 375°F oven for 12 minutes. Makes 6 dozen cookies.

WHOLESOME PEANUT BUTTER COOKIES

Whole wheat flour and honey in place of sugar make the healthy difference.

1 cup peanut oil
1 cup peanut butter, unhomogenized
1 cup honey
1 tsp. salt
1 tsp. baking soda
2 eggs
1 tsp. vanilla
2 cups whole wheat flour

74

Mix oil and peanut butter. Add honey, salt, and soda. Stir well. Add eggs and vanilla. When well blended add flour. Drop by teaspoonfuls ónto lightly oiled cookie sheets. Press down with a floured fork, if desired. Bake in a 350°F oven 10 to 11 minutes. Let cool on pans several minutes.

OLD FASHION PEANUT BRITTLE

If you've never tasted fresh, homemade peanut brittle, you've really never tasted peanut brittle!

2 cups white sugar
1 cup white corn syrup
1/4 cup water
2 cups raw Spanish peanuts
1 tsp. baking soda
1 tsp. salt
1 tsp. vinegar

Combine sugar, corn syrup and water. Cook to soft ball stage, 236°F on candy thermometer. Add peanuts and cook until mixture turns dark. Remove from heat. Add baking soda, salt and vinegar. Stir well. Pour onto buttered cookie sheet. Cool and break into pieces. Makes 2 pounds.

⋙ Snacks ⋘

Face it! We are a nation of unrestrained snackers. But why let the afterschool bunch fill up on junk when you can provide treats that are inexpensive and pack protein. With so many peanut butter cravers running rampant, the solution of "what's to snack on" is half solved. And, peanut butter ranks very near the top in at least six nutritional categories: food energy, fats necessary to maintain body balance, protein, phosphorous, thiamine and niacin. A look at the diagram below might convince even a teenager to go for peanuts before potato chips.

Grams of protein per 3 oz. serving of peanuts.

Jellies
.1 gram

Pretzels
9.8 grams

Cottage
Cheese
17.0 grams

Potato
Chips
5.3 grams

Frankfurters
(all meat)
13.1 grams

Peanuts
26 grams

Peanut
Butter
27.8 grams

There is no excuse for empty calories if you remember the peanut. Try some of these goober goodies.

PEANUT PARTY TREAT

2 cups cocktail peanuts
1 cup oats
1/2 cup dark seedless raisins
1 tbs. grated orange peel
1/4 cup honey

1 tbs. melted butter
2 tsp. vanilla
1 tsp. cinnamon
1/4 tsp. nutmeg
1/4 tsp. cloves

78   Toss together peanuts, oats, raisins and orange peel. Combine honey, butter, vanilla, cinnamon, nutmeg and cloves. Pour over peanut mixture. Toss until evenly coated. Spread on a large baking sheet with sides. Bake in 250°F oven 30 minutes. Stir several times. Makes 4 cups.

NATURE'S MUNCH

Thoroughly combine 1 cup sunflower seeds with 1 cup peanuts (try 1/2 cup dry roasted and 1/2 cup cocktail) and 1 cup raisins (perhaps 1/2 cups light and 1/2 cup dark). Place in a covered container in an easy-to-reach place.

PEANUT APPLE TOASTIES

Tempt non-breakfast eaters with this luscious combination. It makes a good snack anytime of day.

2 slices bread, toasted and buttered (raisin bread is terrific)
2 tbs. peanut butter
1/2 apple, sliced
lemon juice
1 tsp. brown sugar
cinnamon

79

Spread peanut butter on one side of each slice of toasted bread. Dip apple slices in lemon juice. Arrange on top of peanut butter. Sprinkle apple slices with brown sugar and cinnamon. Place on baking sheet. Broil 3 to 5 minutes or until lightly browned. Makes 2 servings.

PIZZA SPINNERS

Two favorites join forces for a terrific snack. Keep the ingredients on hand for the after-school-refrigerator-raiders.

1 English muffin, split, toasted and buttered
2 tbs. peanut butter
2 tbs. canned pizza sauce
2 sliced bologna, cut into julienne strips
2 tbs. shredded pizza cheese

80

Spread peanut butter and then pizza sauce on English muffin halves. Top with bologna and pizza cheese. Heat in 400°F oven 5 to 10 minutes or until pizzas are hot and cheese is melted. Makes 2 servings.

Did you know the United States produces 1/10th of the world's peanut crop, mostly in Georgia, Alabama, Texas, Oklahoma, Virginia, North Carolina and Florida?

PEPPERY PEANUTS

These and Peanut Party Treats, page 78, make great gifts. Pack them in a pretty container, perhaps an interesting glass jar, attach a bow and you'll be a happy gift-giver.

2 cups cocktail peanuts
1 tbs. melted butter
1 tbs. rosemary leaves, crushed
1/2 tsp. thyme, crushed
1/2 tsp. marjoram leaves, crushed
1/2 tsp. garlic salt
1/4 tsp. cayenne pepper

Toss all ingredients together. Place on a jelly roll pan. Bake in a preheated 350°F oven 10 minutes, stirring once. Makes 2 cups.

PEPPY PEANUT BUTTER

The peanut butter purist may not want to experiment, but serve him this once and count on him asking for it again.

1 cup peanut butter
1/4 cup mayonnaise or salad dressing
1/4 cup sweet pickle relish
1/4 cup crumbled cooked bacon
2 tbs. minced green onion

82

Mix together all ingredients. Use as a spread on raisin or whole wheat bread. Makes about 1-1/2 cups.

PEANUTTY CHEESE SPREAD

A change of pace for lunch box sandwiches and delicious broiled on cocktail rye for an easy hors d'oeuvre.

2 cups (8 ozs.) shredded Cheddar cheese
1 cup (4 ozs.) shredded Swiss cheese
1/2 cup chopped cocktail peanuts
1/2 cup mayonnaise or salad dressing
2 tbs. chopped pimiento
1 tbs. minced green onion
1 tsp. prepared mustard

In a bowl combine cheeses and peanuts. Mix together mayonnaise, pimiento, green onion and mustard. Stir into cheese mixture. Spread on rye or whole wheat bread. May be grilled or broiled open-face. Makes 1-3/4 cups.

NATURAL SWEET TREAT

Pop into lunch bags and don't say a word about how wholesome they are!

1/3 cup honey

1/2 cup nonfat dry milk

1/2 cup crunchy peanut butter

84   Mix honey and peanut butter in bowl. Stir in dry milk a little at a time until thoroughly blended. Shape into narrow roll. Wrap in waxed paper. Chill. Cut into 1-inch pieces. Wrap in plastic and twist the ends tightly.

EASY PEANUT BUTTER FUDGE

1 cup peanut butter

1-1/4 cups nonfat milk solids

1 cup corn syrup

1-1/4 cups sifted powdered sugar

Measure ingredients into large bowl. Mix well, then knead. Form into small balls. Makes about 2 pounds.

GO GO SHAKE

Even very young school children can make this treat for a friend.

1 small banana
1/4 cup smooth peanut butter

1/2 pt. vanilla ice cream
1 cup milk

Break banana into blender container. Blend until smooth. Add peanut butter, ice cream and milk. Blend until smooth. Makes 2 servings.

NUTTY COCOA

1/3 cup cocoa
1/2 cup sugar

4 cups milk
1 cup peanut butter

Combine cocoa, sugar and a dash of salt in saucepan. Blend in 1/4 cup milk and peanut butter. Stir in remaining milk. Heat to simmering. Serve in mugs. Also good served well chilled. Makes about 6 servings.

PEANUT SWIRL

2 tbs. peanut butter
2 graham cracker squares
1 tbs. strawberry, pineapple or orange yogurt
nutmeg

Spread peanut butter on graham crackers and swirl on yogurt. spinkle with nutmeg.

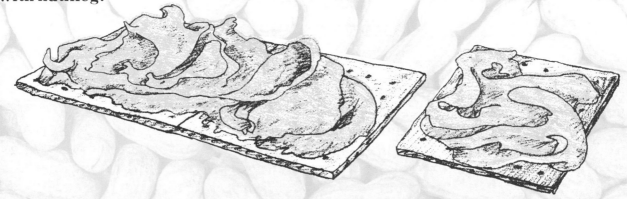

Index

87